Praise from others for *Spirit Soundings...*

"I proudly endorse David Reid Brown's book," without reservation. As a recently retired Navy Chaplain and having served on four different Navy combatant vessels with four overseas deployments, including deployments to the Persian Gulf, I identify with every word David reveals in his journal. Not only do I know David as a fellow Navy Chaplain, but I also know him to be a humble man of great character, and I call him friend. *Spirit Soundings* is a window allowing us to see David's conviction of faith and his commitment to serve God's people in the Sea Services. If you are a greenhorn (little or no experience) on the matters of life onboard a Navy combatant ship, this book will present a vivid, day-to-day, summary of a then young Chaplain's spiritual life during his first shipboard assignment. If you are an old salt, like me, you will be touched by the author's ability to paint the picture with imaginative words and candor; so much so, that as I read this journal, it caused me to laugh, cry, and pray all in one sitting. The stories are simple, yet deeply immersed in the Eternal.

"The message within this book is simple: "In the beginning, the Spirit of God hovered upon the surface of the waters...", and today each of us can still encounter God there. Be inspired far beyond par! Read it and expect the unexpected."

–Captain Brenda BradleyDavila, CHC, USN (Ret.)
Colorado Springs, Colorado

It has been my privilege to know David Reid Brown and his family since 2010. Dave is a man of God that I respect, one whom hears from God and has the courage to be God's messenger. I am certain that *Spirit Soundings* is going to challenge each person to a renewed sense of openness to the voice of God. *Spirit Soundings* will show you that God is always speaking and directing by his Spirit and it will challenge you to expect to hear from Him."

Lea

D1432158

Spirit Soundings provides a unique and first-hand view of military chaplaincy yet, I believe, also has an appeal to the un-churched / seekers, especially young people who may feel life circumstances are pushing them beyond their own limits and resources, and are seeking God actively or unknowingly. In *Spirit Soundings,* David Reid Brown gives us the result of "sailing into a hazardous world" as a newly deployed Navy Chaplain. These pages offer a spiritually mature, sometimes striking, often moving account of a man of God called to offer comfort and counsel to young men and women at sea. It's a compelling, deeply honest and wise read.

–Rev. Denise Mosher
Salem, Oregon

Through *Spirit Soundings*, Chaplain David Reid Brown introduces readers to the exciting reality that God is at work in every thing that happens. David is a man of great spiritual fervor, who exemplifies the high ideals of Christian living and giving. I have known him since he entered the ministry twenty-three years ago, when I served as the pastor of an AME church in Roanoke, VA. Knowing him has been an inspiration to me because of who he is and I consider him to be my 'Best Friend and Brother'.

–Rev. Frank W. Saunders
Clayton, North Carolina

SPIRIT SOUNDINGS

Volume II: The Patriot's Call

A Chaplain's Journal of Life at Sea

DAVID REID BROWN

Copyright © 2016 by David Reid Brown

SPIRIT SOUNDINGS Volume II: The Patriot's Call
A Chaplain's Journal of Life At Sea
by David Reid Brown

Printed in the United States of America.

ISBN 9781498479981

All rights reserved solely by the author. The author guarantees all contents are original and do not infringe upon the legal rights of any other person or work. No part of this book may be reproduced in any form without the permission of the author. The views expressed in this book are not necessarily those of the publisher.

Unless otherwise indicated, Scripture.quotations taken from the New International Version (NIV). Copyright © 1973, 1978, 1984, 2011 by Biblica, Inc.™. Used by permission. All rights reserved.

Scripture.quotations taken from the King James Version (KJV) – public domain.

www.xulonpress.com

DEDICATION

To Almighty God:

The One who makes all such stories possible.

ACKNOWLEDGEMENTS

I would like to thank the families of Information Systems Technician Second Class (Surface Warfare) Kris R. Bishundat and Machinist Mate Fireman Patrick D. White for allowing me to share the story of your son, brother, and Sailor.

Dr. Larry Keefauver, for his invaluable work and wisdom and all it contributed to getting this book published.

Master Chief Machinist Mate (Surface Warfare) Scott Maretich, who refreshed my memory of and fondness for Steam Engineering and "Snipes".

Mrs. Tina Martinez, for her assistance with the portions of the book that required Spanish to English translation.

PREFACE

People are my details. Discerning and then attending to the needs of others have always been my center of gravity. Through my professional career, first as a civilian pastor and most recently as a Navy Chaplain, I have embraced the fact that I was created to be a care provider. Many of my colleagues build programs that meet the broad range of needs in our institution while others build policies and procedures that govern our conduct and allow for the efficient flow of administration. As for me,

I build people.

Here is how: *God took my innate "wiring" and placed it on a career path through which it could be used to bring out what is best in others.*

My mother told me one thing before I departed for my first tour as a Navy Chaplain: "Write it down!" I suppose that she sensed some very unique experiences in my future would be worth recording. However, I never took her advice. I was just too enamored with the sensory aspects— sights, sounds, and sojourn— of the experience to be bothered with "pen and paper." So, all of my experiences during my first tour of duty at Twentynine Palms, California and the following one at Great Lakes, Illinois, now exist in ever-fading memories.

My change of heart came upon accepting orders to my first ship assignment to the USS SHREVEPORT (LPD-12). I suppose that every Navy Chaplain's dream is to go to sea; it took me nearly six years to fulfill mine.

From my very first day aboard ship, I had this overwhelming sense that this experience was going to be very special—even remarkable—thus, worthy of recording. Hats off to a mother's wisdom!

At this writing, there are over 800 Active Duty and Reserve Component Navy Chaplains, each one with the ability to pen a far more interesting story. Nonetheless, this one is mine; it is a junior chaplain's chronicle of his initial experience at sea.

My prayer is that God would use this account to open
or deepen His relationship with you.
- David Reid Brown

TABLE OF CONTENTS

They took soundings and found that the water was
a hundred and twenty feet deep.
A short time later they took soundings again
and found it was ninety feet deep.
Fearing that we would be dashed against the rocks,
they dropped four anchors from the stern and prayed for daylight.
(Acts 27:28-29)

1

ATLANTIC CROSSING

The Journey begins

19 September 2001
Norfolk, VA

We arrived early at the Pier 5 Naval Station Norfolk so we could beat the throng of sailors, cargo trucks, and forklifts that would eventually congest access to the pier later that morning. My wife was beside me while my son sat in his toddler seat in the back of the car.

It was deployment day.

The day that both sailors and family members take months to prepare for but still makes us feel unready. Those feelings were exacerbated in the wake of the national emergency precipitated by the attack on America.

I got out of the car and checked the back seat and trunk to ensure I had every bag I packed. My wife still asked the obligatory, "Are you *sure* you have everything?" I was, but I checked anyway. I dropped my bags and started with my son, reaching around the small of his neck with one hand and gently resting my other on his right shoulder. I leaned forward and kissed him on his head.

"Daddy loves you, man!" I repeated the kiss but on his cheek this time. "Daddy loves you very much. Be a good boy for Momma, okay?"

I was just close enough for him to reach into my shirt and pull out my dog tags, as was his custom. He loved the jingling sound of the metal tag against the chain.

"Dadda," he repeated as he tugged.

"Be a good boy for Momma. Daddy loves you."

As I pulled away, he cracked a broad smile, which was half gums, half teeth, all the while clapping his hands in excitement. He could not understand the moment.

I turned to my wife, kissed her, and we gave each other a good hug. We pledged our love, hugged and kissed again, and reassured each other that everything would be all right. Just as I picked up my bags and headed for the gate to the pier, I told her to check her email. I would be in touch. There were no tears—at least at that time. We had done this before when we were stationed in California. The Lord blessed us there and we survived. It was just the gravity of our circumstances that made this time feel different.

Once aboard ship, I made it to my stateroom and took a moment to pray and collect myself. A couple hours later, I changed into my coveralls and headed for the Pilot House because we were about to get underway. There would be several other ships heading out to sea before us: THEODORE ROOSEVELT, BATAAN, VELLA GULF, and WHIDBEY ISLAND to mention a few. The atmosphere in the Pilot House, which was crowded with sailors manning their posts, was very tense but also solemn.

At exactly 1100, the captain turned to the Officer-of-the-Deck (OOD) and said,

"Officer of the Deck! Call 'Underway.'"

"Aye, Aye, Sir!" The OOD in turn ordered the boatswain mate to do the same.

Boats keyed the microphone and blew one short fluttering whistle of his pipe, which could be heard throughout the ship via the 1MC intercom. ***"UNDERWAY! SHIFT COLORS!"***, announced the boatswain mate. The Junior Officer-of-the Watch pulled the lever controlling the ship's whistle and it blew a long, resounding blast signaling to everyone as far as it could be heard that we were pulling away from the pier.

The media, CNN as well as local affiliates, were covering our departure. I left the Pilot House and walked out to the bridge wing to watch. Sailors gathering on the starboard side of the Flight Deck waved goodbye to loved ones standing at the end of the pier. As we proceeded out towards the Chesapeake Bay, the captain ordered some patriotic music be played over the 1MC. First, "God bless America" then Aaron Copeland's "Fanfare for the Common Man." It was quite inspiring—the gallant music and the parade of ships leaving port—we were off to do our nation's bidding. Once the parade of ships completed their transit through the bay, the ships that were attached to the ROOSEVELT Battle Group headed east to commence their crossing. We, however, headed south for Morehead City, North Carolina to embark our main battle component—The United States Marines.

The Journey Begins

Let us pray.
"Be strong and take courage! Do not be afraid or be dismayed, for I the Lord your God, am with you wherever you go."[1]

Lord, as our journey continues, we have discovered that its parameters have changed, the scope has constricted its focus, and the stakes are much higher. These variations have contributed to the slight inflation of our anxiety and apprehension.

You know our hearts tonight; our secret thoughts are not hidden from you. Though today's departure was difficult, we did not leave port empty-handed. We bear the affection of loved ones and ride the crest of prayers and well wishes of the American people.

By faith we sail into the unknown. The on-load plan is set, the charts and track are accurate, and the transit time is unchanged. Yet, we know little

---

[1] Joshua 1:9

more than it is our time to relieve the Watch.
The only thing that is clear is that we must go.

And go we shall; let it be with your blessing, let it be with your protection,
let it be with your peace.

"Be strong and take courage. Do not fear or be dismayed, for I the
Lord your God, am with you wherever you go."

Amen.

20 September

I observed that the crew was a bit down in the mouth most of the way down to Morehead City. That all changed once we pulled into port. The Marines from the 26th Marine Expeditionary Unit (MEU) were pulling up in buses that had been chartered from Camp LeJeune, North Carolina. We trained all spring and summer with the 26th MEU throughout the Atlantic and the Caribbean. These were our brothers and sisters-in-arms and we knew them well. Just the site of them off-loading their sea bags, personnel, and heavy equipment put a spark in the crew. Once again, the news media was present but they were restricted to an area on the pier about fifty yards from the ship. Nevertheless, they flagged down any Sailor or Marine that would give a sound bite or interview. We were instant celebrities who in all actuality were just doing our duties.

At dusk, with the on-load of Marines and machinery complete, it was time to depart and head east. An impromptu flotilla of speedboats and other small watercraft joined us on either side of the ship. They were our unofficial escort as we made our way out of port, exchanging waves and greetings along the way. I made it down to the Flight Deck so I could get the best view of these well-wishers. 1st LT Adams was there and we struck up a conversation about the great send-off we were receiving. At the mouth of the Bouge Sound, where Morehead City inlet and the Atlantic Ocean met, we stopped talking. A group of people was lined up onshore about four hundred yards off our starboard side—close enough to see their faces—waving their hands and flags. The ship gave three short blasts of its whistle to acknowledge their presence. My heart was as full as First Lieutenant's eyes. At the edge of the sand at the lip of the inlet, a group of children stood encircling a message written in the sand, which was obviously directed to a crewmember:

WE LOVE YOU DADDY

I drew a deep breath, and then exhaled to help dissipate the lump of emotion building in my throat. No words were necessary. We just wanted to soak up this moment when we could feel the whole hope and support of the entire nation behind us. It would be the last time we would see America and her flag-waving citizens for six months.

Atlantic Crossing

Let us pray.

Gracious Lord, we thank you for the assemblage of Marines and sailors who comprise Gator Team 12. The will of our nation has been galvanized to see justice exacted upon the enemy and we represent the long arm of the law. This is the expectation and responsibility we carry as we cross the Atlantic.

Our journey comes with an inordinate burden placed upon our loved ones who, while understanding the nature of our mission, undoubtedly will burn the midnight oil praying on our behalf. And so we crossover with a greater purpose; we cancel the myth of the standard six-month deployment and accept the unwritten script awaiting us on the other side.

We crossover:
from familiar shores to distant seas,
from training exercises to the basic execution of our duty,
from war-gaming to engaging a real world threat.

We crossover: in faith, not knowing what the future holds but knowing the One who holds the future.

Lord bless our crossing over the deep expanse of the ocean with each day drawing us closer to an abiding dependence upon you.

This we pray in you Awesome Name,

Amen.

21 September
300 miles down, 3500 to go

With one day of sailing under our belts, roughly three-hundred miles, the crew began to settle into their normal shipboard routine: Reveille at 0600, Marine PT on the Flight Deck, breakfast, Officer's Call, Prayer Meeting, ship-wide painting, cleaning and repairs. Our first port visit would be Rota, Spain but that was at least ten days away.

The USS SHREVEPORT (LPD-12), which was part of the "Gator Navy", was an Amphibious Transport Dock whose sole design and function was to project Marines and their tactical assets ashore. It was equipped with a Flight Deck for helicopters and a Well Deck inside that could be partially filled with sea water allowing the smaller Landing Craft Unit (LCU) within the well to transport the Marines and equipment. We were transiting along with our two sister "gators", the USS BATAAN and the USS WHIDBEY ISLAND. As an ensemble we comprised the BATAAN Amphibious Ready Group.

Morale about the crew was still very high. For most, including myself, it was the first Trans-Atlantic crossing. The level of excitement would not wane anytime soon. Besides, something quite visceral happens to sailors when they depart the shore and land disappears. In the back of their minds they realize they are not in control of their environments and anything could happen. The ship is their only lifeline. They become acutely aware of the elements surrounding them: the incessant wind sweeping across the ship from forward to aft, water that stretches so far it becomes the horizon, and the open canopy of the day and night sky. In this sense, SHREVEPORT was both warship and ark. Fortunately, these elements were with us since our departure and kept the ship at a gentle pitch and roll. However, the North

Atlantic was fabled for its foul weather and heavy seas. The "salty"—experienced—sailors could tell harrowing sea stories about how even the largest vessels would mercilessly bob like a cork, the crew wither and become green in the gills with sea sickness during heavy seas.

26 September
About halfway there

We had been underway for a week and I had already begun executing the plan for the Command Religious Program (CRP). One of my first undertakings was to review the religious support plan for the religious holidays that would occur over the next three months, namely Rosh Hashanah, Ramadan, Hanukah and Christmas. Providing support for the non-Protestant crewmembers basically consisted of having a designated command sponsored Lay Reader from that particular faith group. About once a week though, a Catholic Priest from the USS BATAAN was scheduled to fly over on the Holy HELO to conduct the Mass. A Rabbi and Imam for Jewish and Muslim personnel respectively would only be available once we arrived in the Mediterranean Sea.

In addition to those responsibilities, I was normally tasked with being an advisor for specific national and cultural celebrations such as Columbus Day, Thanksgiving Day, and Martin Luther King, Jr. Day as well as Native American, Hispanic, and African-American Heritage Months. On a regular basis, the CRP consisted of a daily prayer meeting, Bible Study, and worship services throughout the week. Admittedly, I am biased:

I believe religious faith should be at the center of everything we pursue in life.

Of course, not everyone shared that opinion and it was his or her right to do so. It was simply more encouraging to see sailors and Marines who had the switch of their spiritual life in the "ON" position.

The one collateral duty I had was as the ship's Library Officer. I was responsible for maintaining the spaces containing the Library Multi-Media Resource Center or LMRC. The LMRC contained the library and computer room and also served as memorials dedicated to two SHREVEPORT sailors. The Library was named after Fireman Patrick D. White, a native of Holly Hill, South Carolina, who was tragically shot to death over the summer while on Leave. Fireman White had just been in the Navy for about five months and aboard ship for two. The Computer Room was dedicated to Petty Officer Second Class Kris R. Bishundat from Waldorf, Maryland. "Bish," as his peers affectionately knew him, transferred in the spring to the Pentagon but was killed in the terrorist attack on September 11th.

During deployment, a ship's library and computer rooms were the most widely used spaces next to the Mess Deck and contributed greatly to the morale and welfare of the crew. Therefore, these spaces were a living tribute to the vitality these shipmates displayed while serving aboard SHREVEPORT.

Our good fortune was about to run out, putting an end to our smooth transit thus far. The north Atlantic was about to clearly demonstrate how it received its infamous reputation of creating some of the heaviest seas known to mariners. Our own weather forecasters predicted the remnants of Hurricane Humberto would chase us all the way to Europe increasing the seas that surrounded us. The docile two to four foot waves escalated to seven to ten feet amplifying the pitch and roll of the ship practically negating any effort to stand stable or walk in a straight line. During heavy seas, there was only one position that brought the queasy stomach peace: horizontal. Without the aid of medication, the best way to appease seasickness was to lie down flat. For some reason, this position restored the equilibrium and told a Sailor's sense of balance that everything was okay. Silence and inactivity pervaded the ship during heavy seas and only sailors with the strongest stomachs or the longest sea legs could withstand the pronounced to and fro motion. I took a tour. The Mess Deck were all quiet. The berthing areas, both Navy and Marine were all quiet. Even those who were standing the Watch were quiet because talking seemed to aggravate the feeling of nausea. *Why was I faring so well?* It took me nearly a year, with several intermittent deployments, for my body to assimilate to moderately heavy seas. However, I remember all too well when horizontal was the only way I could get through a workday. Indeed, the Lord made a brilliant design when he drafted our physical blueprint. At times like this I was convinced his original intention for our natural environment was *terra firma*.

28 September
Two Days from Spain

The seas had settled once again as Humberto, now just a tropical depression, turned northeast while we headed due east. Our transit was reaching its conclusion and the closer we fared towards Spain the better the conditions became. Just two days from port, the skies became clear and calm and the sea as smooth as glass. As far as the eye could see there was barely a ripple. The ocean was totally undisturbed save the parting waters created by the bow plowing through it and the wake left by the ship's propellers. We were sailing through a tranquil aquatic environment whose serenity surpassed anything we had experienced along the way.

Seeing that it was too nice to stay inside the ship, I headed out to the Flight Deck for some out-and-about ministry to engage sailors in their informal conversations. Sailors call it something entirely different though— smoking and joking—a time to hang out, chat, gripe, laugh, whatever came to mind. There was an art to approaching them on the deckplates of the ship. Normally, if they were in a small group or standing alone but close to a group it was probably a good opportunity to interact with them. However, some sailors opted to be alone in solitary places on the outskirts of the Flight Deck. That is when it got tricky. A Sailor who was standing alone most likely had something on his mind but did not necessarily desire to share it with someone else. Sailors are known to be alone in their thoughts; they stare out into the open ocean almost in a trance-like state for a half-hour or so never seeking company or conversation. So, I had to be able to read the sailor's mood through body language and other non-verbal cues. Once savvy, I knew which ones to approach and which ones had "Do Not Disturb" posted. All crewmembers, from the captain to the most junior Sailor, practiced being alone and derived a measure of personal peace that often could not be expressed in words. In its own way, the sea could counsel sailors and in a sense bore a significant part of my daily workload.

Later that evening, God provided quite a spectacle. Our course and speed was such, the ship's wake was directly in line with the setting sun, still brilliant in its waning effervescence. In front of the ship was a full moon, not as brilliant, but gaining as the dominant figure in the dusk. The open-air clarity of the sky simultaneously enhanced the visual effect of both celestial bodies and attracted many other crewmembers to the Flight Deck equipped with video and digital cameras to record the event. In my mind, it was divine recompense for the day we missed due to the tempest and provided fitting inspiration for the evening prayer.

God's Peace

Let us pray.

Gracious Lord, tonight we thank you for the providence of your peace in our lives. Your peace gives us patience to endure our rising concerns and anxieties.

*It calms the psychological swells so that our thoughts
do not close in and consume us.*

*It speaks quietly to our heart and reminds us that you are the keeper
of our souls and caretaker of our loved ones.*

*It touches those empty times when we may feel a bit lonely and reassures us
that, with You, we are never alone.*

*Your peace is there for the asking, abides with the willing, and satisfies
beyond understanding. May it ever saturate our spirits with your
supernatural essence!*

This we ask in your Holy Name,

Amen.

30 September

From: CHAPS@SHREVEPORT
To: RB@HOME

Subject: Last Day in the Atlantic (for a while)

Hey!

Our twelve-day stretch across the ocean is coming to an end. We have been blessed to have the Lord's favor with us in many ways, particularly in the calm seas we have experienced.

It was a great day at worship! The numbers were down a bit—sixteen—but we had a rich, full service that was blessed by the Lord. The CO of the Marines as well as our XO were in attendance again. Even our medical officer showed up—something he has been promising to do for a while.

I am getting ready to go out and do some PT on the Flight Deck. It is too nice to do it in the fitness room. I will send off another message this evening before I hit the rack. Remember, we are soon to be five hours ahead of you in time difference.

Take care!

Love,
Chaps

About 2000

We were scheduled to arrive at the Naval Station in Rota, Spain the next afternoon and even though it was going to be a brief twenty-four-hour port visit, the crew was excited to get off the ship. I knew I had to make the most of this time by heading to the commissary to pick up some extra snack items and the uniform shop to purchase a new pair of boots. I also was anxious to see how well the pre-paid phone card I purchased from the ship's store would work.

This last day at sea was the best of all weather-wise: crystal clear skies, temperatures in the seventies, light winds, and a smooth-as-glass ocean all day long. That is why I headed to the Flight Deck to get out and PT. At night we were bathed in brilliant moonlight from a full moon. What a fitting end to a wonderful Sunday!

Once Liberty was sounded, I planned to make contact with Chaplain Atticus Taylor, an AME Chaplain stationed at the naval hospital. Since I did not have his email, my visit was probably going to be a total surprise. I did not know him as well as my other colleagues so there were not going to be any dinner plans to negotiate. Besides, I promised ENS Luckie that I would have dinner with him in town—a promise I was going to keep.

I volunteered to cook again, this time it would be breakfast for the crew in the morning on the Mess Deck. I would be taking up the "Cook-to-Order" spot on the mess line, fixing up hundreds of eggs—fried, scrambled, sunny side-up, omelets, etc. The officers and chief petty officers would sometimes cook for the crew as an act of appreciation. Even the captain took his turn slinging hash, a motivating morale booster for any Sailor in the chow line.

"TATTOO, TATTOO! LIGHTS OUT IN FIVE MINUTES! STAND BY FOR THE EVENING PRAYER."

Faithful to the End (coming into Spain)

Let us pray.

Gracious Lord, our hearts are filled with praise and thanksgiving as we encounter the termination of our initial transit across the sea. Allow us to recount how faithful you have been:

In providing for our needs each and every day, watching over loved ones, and restoring our strength when it often ran low: You were faithful, completely faithful.

*In sustaining us throughout the journey, keeping major storms at bay, and
sea swells at a low-long rhythm:
You were faithful, completely faithful.*

*In keeping morale high, injuries minor and few, for fostering
a cooperative spirit between sailors and Marines:
You were faithful, completely faithful.*

*In providing this port visit, the opportunity for tax-free pay,
and holding the future right in the palm of your hand:
You are faithful, completely faithful.*

*Lord we could go on all night listing every little way you have been faithful
towards us. Suffice to say, our debt of gratitude, which we could never repay,
is best summed up by the words of this hymn:*

*"Great is Thy Faithfulness, great is thy faithfulness;
Morning by morning new mercies I see.
All I have needed your hand has provided.
Great is thy faithfulness, Lord unto me."*

Amen.

**"TAPS, TAPS, LIGHTS OUT! ALL HANDS TURN TO YOUR
BUNKS. MAINTAIN SILENCE ABOUT THE DECKS. TAPS!"**

2

ROTA, SPAIN

Arriving in the "Old World"

01 October 2001

As we were pulling into port, the USS KEARSARGE passed us on the port side on its way home after completing its six-month deployment. I marveled at them and thought, *Those lucky sailors! They got the last real MED (Mediterranean) Cruise for a while.* The typical MED Cruise included seeing most of southern Europe—Spain, France, Italy, and Greece—but also places like Malta, Turkey, and Israel. These were the standard highlights sailors would be treated to by traveling east to the Old World—but not this time! The world had changed and so did the possibility of seeing these places. We were even told that we would be restricted to the naval base once we pulled into port. Security would be tight and tensions high. Still, many crewmembers, including myself, were excited because it was our first time we had ever been to Europe.

The port at Rota had several ships, all Spanish, docked at the piers, which seemed to be frigates and amphibious transports. Three more ships, all American, were about to join them: BATAAN, SHREVEPORT, and WHIDBEY ISLAND. When we arrived around 1300, the captain made it official: On-base Liberty only, for all sailors and Marines. The threat level in the wake of the attack was still very high and keeping the crew on the base was a smart and safe decision.

"LIBERTY CALL, LIBERTY CALL! LIBERTY CALL FOR DUTY SECTIONS 2, 4, AND 6. LIBERTY EXPIRES AT 0600 ON 02 OCTOBER."

ENS Luckie and I were heading off the ship to go onto base together but before I could get to the brow, the command chaplain from the naval station chapel and his deputy were standing right there in uniform waiting to greet me. Although it was a pleasant and flattering surprise, their presence immediately made me feel underdressed. The only chaplain I had planned to meet with was Chaplain Taylor. They obviously realized I was heading off the ship to go on Liberty but they graciously extended an invitation to tour the chapel and join them for dinner. I politely declined because I wanted to hang with Derby for the evening. Still, I thought it would be a good idea to stop by the chapel.

The command chaplain was good enough to offer us a ride to the main side of the base. What I observed on the way seemed very familiar: the old Spanish mission style white stucco buildings with terra cotta roofs, the warm, inviting, and slightly arid climate, and the tall and proliferate date palm trees dotting the entire route. Rota seemed like the San Diego of Europe. We were grateful for the ride that dropped us off at the center of the base. We had to hurry, though, to locate an ATM machine. There were literally thousands of sailors and Marines from all three ships that had the same thing on their minds. Any delay in locating one meant waiting in a long line just to access some cash.

My first mission was to locate a decent place to eat. Derby and I decided on pizza, which was actually pretty good. We caught a ride back to the pier on the base shuttle bus and when we arrived, there was a big banquet set up right beside the ship. The Morale, Welfare, and Recreation (MWR) or "The Fun Guys" from the naval station had set up some entertainment for that evening alongside the ship. "Bar-b-Que and Beer on The Pier" they called it. Basically, it was a big picnic serving all-u-can eat steaks, smoked sausage, hot dogs, hamburgers, and fixins. The CO dropped the drinking age on the pier from twenty-one to nineteen, which encouraged many sailors and Marines to stay put. Besides, keeping inebriated personnel in a secure and controlled area promoted safety and significantly reduced the risk of illegal, immoral, or just plain dumb incidents while on Liberty. Loud Rap, Rock-n-Roll, and Country music was played late into the night.

3

DEPARTING ROTA
The Journey continues

02 October 2001

I had the opportunity early in the morning to visit the BATAAN moored at an adjacent pier for a meeting with the command chaplain and Sixth Fleet Chaplain. The two chaplains from the WHIDBEY ISLAND also joined us. Of the many things we discussed one item was a main concern:

How do we provide Force Protection for sailors and Marines
who participate in COMRELs?

The Sixth Fleet Chaplain suggested we have a plan in place because there was a good chance that any country we visited could have elements who could manipulate our goodwill by embarrassing or harming our personnel during any COMREL project.

The Strait of Gibraltar

We departed Rota in the early afternoon and arrived at the mouth of the Strait of Gibraltar just before dusk. We had to wait there for several hours as other ships began their passage through the strait. The daylight had faded when we proceeded towards the strait. The plan was for a nighttime transit to minimize the security risk. Oil tankers and cargo vessels transiting east and west were pretty heavy through the strait. The Marines took up positions on the Flight Deck with various weapons systems, using night vision binoculars to scan the surface of the water in every direction to identify potential threats. In the wake of the events of September 11th, there was a heightened sense that anything could happen at any time. The captain directed me to delay the Evening Prayer until we exited the strait and stood down our security watches. That meant a late night's prayer sometime past midnight.

03 October
0147

Safe Passage

Let us pray.

Gracious Lord, we praise you for a safe passage through the Strait of Gibraltar tonight. Thank you for the strength and vigilance you provided to all watch-standers, from the Main Spaces to the Signal Bridge, the Pilot House to Aft Steering, everyone's efforts contributed to a successful passage.

Tonight, we have been given a safe passage: a new opportunity to prepare, train and execute, another chance to do and be our personal and professional best, a new opportunity to respect each other.

It is a new passage even for those who have come this way before. Their experiences may give them a slight edge against the unknown but that margin is far too slim to expect that this journey will replicate previous ones.

Lord, please do not allow us to squander this moment through selfishness, inattention, or carelessness. Do not let something as prevalent as fatigue or disruptive as poor planning compromise the mission or cause serious injury or worse.

O Lord, we transit a new passage filled with possibilities. Make one of them to know you, to open our hearts and inquire what you require of our lives, and to experience the fullness of your mercy, pardon, and peace.

Amen.

1147
From: CHAPS@SHREVEPORT
To: RB@HOME

Subject: I SAW AFRICA LAST NIGHT!

Hey!

We passed through the Strait of Gibraltar from last night (2200-0200). The full moon illuminated the sea and sky well enough to look over the coast of Morocco to our starboard and Spain to our port. By the time we reached "The Rock," a dense fog began to roll in and obscured its view. Many Marines and sailors were up late last night just to say they saw two continents at the same time. It was an experience I won't soon forget.

We left Rota around 1400, 0800 your time yesterday. It took hours of floating around until we got the green light to go through the passage. This underway period will be longer than the Atlantic Crossing because it may be a month or more before we come into any port. I will let you know whatever I can about our operations.

I will write more about it later. I tried to write yesterday but the entire ship was under an email blackout. I am going to get as many short messages off every chance I get because you never know when the plug is going to get pulled.

Love you very much! :-)
Chaps

I took a moment to write Chaplain Sydnor so he could inform our Church of the progress of my journey. He quickly forwarded the message:

From: CHSYDNOR@HU
To: Undisclosed-Recipient

Subject: NEWS FROM A DEPLOYED NAVY CHAPLAIN

NEWS FROM CHAPLAIN DAVID BROWN, ONE OF OUR AME
CHAPLAINS DEPLOYED. WILL FORWARD THE ADDRESSES OF
ALL OF OUR DEPLOYED CHAPLAINS THE NEXT DAY OR SO.
CHAPLAIN TAYLOR IS ALSO AN AME CHAPLAIN.

This is a short note to let you know I have made it safely across the ocean. Our first port visit was to Rota, Spain where I immediately met up with Chaplain Taylor. We spent the afternoon talking and sharing our experiences. The following day he paid a visit to my ship, the USS SHREVEPORT. I gave him a quick meeting with the commanding officer and then gave a tour of the library, computer room, and my stateroom. My ship departed Rota later in the day. We passed through the Strait of Gibraltar late last night. Being able two view Europe and Africa at the same time under well-moonlit skies is something I will not soon forget.

"Prayer Changes Things!"

Cal Sydnor, D. Min.
Assistant Professor of Ethics and Religion
The Leadership Institute
Hampton University

4

THE NEW WAR
Conflict defines reality

05 October 2001

I got a surprise email this morning from a friend and colleague back home, Rev. Andrea Cornett-Scott, who was a fellow pastor in southwestern Virginia. Andrea was a natural-born leader and *very* outspoken. In fact, she was so outspoken we nicknamed her Angela Davis, after the prominent political activist from the 1960's.

From: ACSCOTT@HOME
To: CHAPS@SHREVEPORT

Subject: Praying for You

David

I have you in my prayers and think about you all the time, wondering where you were and now I know. Remember, "God is our refuge...a present help in time of trouble."

Your friend,
Andrea, aka, Angela Davis

From: CHAPS@SHREVEPORT
To: ACSCOTT@HOME

Re: Praying for You

Dear Angela,

So good to hear from you! Thanks for remembering me in your prayers but also keep my wife and son lifted up as well. I cannot tell you much about where I am and what we are doing. Just know that I am serving the Lord on the high seas and doing my best to represent our church. Please tell your husband that I said, "Hello."

Sincerely,

David

From: ACSCOTT@HOME
To: CHAPS@SHREVEPORT

Re: Praying for You

Hey! We are praying for the whole Brown Clan. Frank and Cynthia were here a couple of weeks ago. We laughed until we cried. Send me your home address so I can send your wife a note to let her know we are thinking about you all.

Andrea

From: CHAPS@SHREVEPORT
To: ASCOTT@HOME

Re: Praying for You

Andrea

I would love to forward our home address to you but for security reasons I cannot. Email is not as secure as you may think. Some hacker with evil intent could open up a message with my home address and could do whatever they wanted with the information. In short, it would be a threat to my family. If you contact Frank and Cynthia, they would be able to give you that information. Please give them a call and when you do tell them that I am doing great and I said, "Hi."

Thanks again for reaching out!

David

Receiving Rev. Andrea's email refreshed my spirit and reaffirmed that there were those back home who knew where I was, what I was doing, and best of all, had my back. Out of all the uncertainty surrounding us, it was good to know that the bond with my best friends was still a sure thing.

"TATTOO, TATTOO! LIGHTS OUT IN FIVE MINUTES! STAND BY FOR THE EVENING PRAYER."

The Quiet before the Storm

Gracious Lord, thank you for the relative quietness of this evening. Our circumstances seem so still that we can practically see our reflection on the surface. It is times like these that you speak so well into the silence of our souls.

However, the sky is clear and lucid only for a moment and we are not certain what the clouds gathering on the horizon will bring.

Lord, what kind of storm lays ahead us?

Will its winds blow hard enough to create a curdling, incessant howl? Will the rain come down in brief showers or a flash flood that inundates the landscape of our hearts?

*Or will **we** be called upon to provide the thunder and lightning?*

*It is in these quiet moments we learn that only prayer can
cover us through the storm.*

*Prayer is our spiritual Gore-Tex, the foul weather gear that protects against
the punishing elements of life. It provides a shelter to share our hearts with
you and to know that you hear and love us. When we pray, we can open our
ears in willing reverence waiting to receive a Word from you.*

*Lord, whatever storm is headed our way, we are grateful for this quiet moment
that precedes it. Continue to fill it and us with your presence and peace.*

Amen.

07 October
About 1800

The ship's whistle came over the 1MC. By its sound, it was going to be an announcement from the captain:

*"Onboard Shreveport, this is the captain. Let me have your attention.
I want to let you know that the attack has begun. Special forces landed
before dawn in Afghanistan and are engaging in battle as I speak.
Now, I'm not sure how this will affect our underway schedule but for
now we will stay here in the Mediterranean and continue our planned
operations. If you know how to pray, say a prayer this evening for our
warriors in the fight. That is all."*

I went up to the Pilot House to see if I could hear any other information on the attack. When I arrived, I saw ENS Luckie was on Watch as Officer-of-the-Deck. He was outside the ship on the Starboard Bridge Wing peering out over the waters.

"Hey Bro. How's it going?" I asked.

"It's going," he replied.

"Yeah. I know what you mean," I said as I took a position next to him.

We were both pensive, still numbed by the sobering news. Derby decided to break the silence between us.

"Well, we are in it now, Bro," he said.

"You've got that right. We are in it head first!" I said.

"No turning back," he said. "No turning back."

More silence. I sensed Derby wanted some space so I said goodbye, left him at his post in the Pilot House, and headed back downstairs to my stateroom. It was a somber moment throughout the ship.

1910

From: RB@HOME

To: CHAPS@SHREVEPORT

Subject: How are you?

Hi Chaps!

We had a good day today at church. Everyone was remarking how much our son has grown. He was a good boy in church considering it was Communion Sunday. He slept most of the service and he was good throughout the communion service. Dad went to Lynchburg to visit with his aunt who will be ninety-years-old this month and does not look a day over sixty. Her nieces and other relatives are throwing a surprise party today. I felt it was too much for our son after a long day at church. So we are going to make another trip up to Richmond in about two weeks to go visit with Dad's relatives in Lynchburg and Amherst.

I hope all is well out there. Sounds like we have started the attack according to the news on this end and we are waiting to see what is next. Please email when you can.

Love ya very much!

RB

Careful, Considerate, and Conscientious: The "New War" begins

Let us pray.

Sovereign God, we call upon you tonight to make three humble petitions:

Lord, remind us to be careful to pray. The Olive Branch is now hidden and so our prayers must cover those heading into harm's way, those awaiting battle orders, and for all our loved ones whose anxiety is perhaps arcing and dipping along with each news report. Our prayer tonight is for justice, protection, and peace.

Lord, help us be considerate of each other not just as sailors and Marines, but also as human beings that value life and each other. Continue to blur the line between blue side and green side so that all we see are teammates, shipmates, and brothers and sisters in arms. We are all in it headfirst committed to serve like we have trained. Help us step up the level of compassion and care for all aboard SHREVEPORT.

Lord, inspire us to be conscientious. Now that we have clearly demonstrated the ability to strike back, no one is certain where, when, or how it all ends or whether or not we will be directly involved. At this moment of uncertainty, help us consider where we stand with you. These times demand genuine faith—the real deal. No more heads or tails, rabbit's feet, or luck of the draw. It is not enough just to know you exist but to recognize our need, ask for your guidance and gladly be filled with your presence, which brings about true confidence and strength.

O Lord, do hear and honor this triune petition.

Amen.

"TAPS, TAPS, LIGHTS OUT! ALL HANDS TURN TO YOUR BUNKS. MAINTAIN SILENCE ABOUT THE DECKS. TAPS!"

08 October
From: CHAPS@SHREVEPORT
To: RB@HOME

RE: How Are You?

Hey!

I am doing great! Yesterday was another calm, sun-kissed day at sea. After morning service, we had another Steel Beach Picnic. This time they served steaks and pork chops, which were a change from the regular hot dogs and hamburgers. Later, I did some PT, showered, and got ready to prepare my evening prayer. About twenty minutes into writing, the CO announced that the attack had begun. He could not give specifics but I knew the wait was over. Of course, this news changed my perspective about the prayer. In fact, I had to change it three times but I finally received what I was supposed to write. The crew was glued to CNN and interest was high on any info they could get from the broadcast. I sensed the crew was looking for something appropriate in the prayer.

When I went up to the bridge to deliver it, one of the officers asked, "Do you have any inspiring words for us tonight, Chaps?"

"We'll see what the Lord has in store," I answered. It is funny, when the ship realizes the gravity of a moment like last night, they become pin drop silent on the Bridge. The silence continued from "Let us pray" until "Amen" and became utterly deafening after I hung up the 1MC. I have attached a copy to this message.

Praise God for a peaceful and blessed day at church! It always gives me peace to hear that our son had a good day because that means Momma has had one too. I think it was a good decision to stay put, though. Going to Lynchburg could have turned the good into difficult.

Please continue to pray for all of us out here at sea. Keep those who are in the fight lifted up as well as their loved ones. As things heat up, email may be restricted at times. This means there may be hours perhaps as long as days that we will experience email silence. Thanks for your patient understanding about this situation. For now, I will send as much information as often as I can.

Thanks for your loving support. Give our boy a hug and kiss for me today and tell him Dada loves him.

Love,
Chaps

Diligent Service under Duress

Let us pray.

Gracious Lord, our task this evening, as a Navy/Marine Corps team, is to deliver diligent service under duress. We have been hurtled into an environment strewn with question marks. Yet, we hope in some strange way that the unknown will keep us on our toes.

Our challenge has always been to hold the banner of freedom high. Bearing the burden of that privilege has never been easy or ever meant more to America and the world at large.

Lord, we understand why we are here. A clear purpose serves as the blueprint. The building materials—our talent, experience, and capabilities—are sound. Even the will of a supportive nation serves as an ample foundation. Only you can construct a dwelling that can withstand the operational demands of the future. Those demands are dead set to test and tax our strength.

Revive and refresh our minds, bodies, and spirits daily so the caliber of our service to you and our country may never wane or falter.

This we pray in your Mighty Name,

Amen.

5

SOMEWHERE IN THE MED

The blessings of "Snail Mail"

The crew was hungry but not for food. They were thirsty but not for something to drink. Let me explain. We had been anticipating the arrival of our first mail drop since departing Norfolk. There was some sort of delay and it was allegedly sitting in some warehouse in Amsterdam for over a week. Perhaps receiving mail back home may seem like a relatively routine thing, almost inexorable, just step outside and check the box. However, it is a huge deal to deployed sailors and Marines who are deeply connected to whom and what they love. Do not get me wrong, our ship was in the 21st Century and email connectivity with the good people at AOL, Prodigy, Earthlink, Hotmail, etc. and so forth, was not a problem. Make no mistake, anytime we received regular mail at sea it became an "add water and stir" Christmas celebration.

As providence would have it, today mail literally fell out of the sky. We were scheduled for an early hit from a CH-46 helicopter. The 46s were the workhorses of at-sea logistics. They transported everything from passengers to spare parts including mail from ship to shore and between ships. Today's mail drop was in the forefront of many minds; the captain announced it last night on the 1MC and it had been advertised and posted in the Plan of the

Day, not to mention the numerous email reminders from home asking, "Did you get the package yet?"

"FLIGHT QUARTERS! FLIGHT QUARTERS! ALL HANDS MAN YOUR FLIGHT QUARTERS STATIONS!" the Boatswain Mate-of-the-Watch announced over the 1MC. The Flight Deck was cleared of all non-essential personnel and the airmen got into their positions to make preparations for the helicopter's arrival. *"GREEN DECK!"* was called away over the 1MC to alert the ship that the helicopter was cleared to land. Upon arrival, a small working party of Marines unloaded the chopper. Mail at sea is always delivered in large, bright orange, waterproof nylon bags so they would be conspicuous and protect its contents. The Marines made their way from the Flight Deck back inside the ship carrying the bags across the Mess Deck, all to the glances, smiles, and quiet cheers of the crewmembers they passed, and dropped them off at the ship's Post Office. The Postal Clerk, or "PC," began sorting immediately and staging the various sized boxes in the passageway outside of his shop. Today, he was the most popular guy on the ship—hands down! The crew began to form a singular queue along the passageway all the while brimming with anticipation. *"MAIL CALL!"* was passed and the crew was ready to receive.

Being a chaplain, I am not a big proponent of "The Gospel according to St. Nick" but I could not escape the metaphor of the moment: the PC called sailors and Marines by their departments as well as their personal names dispensing the gifts to those who had one on board. Now, that is the down side, most members who lined up did not receive a package or letter on this drop. They would have to wait for the next helicopter flight perhaps tomorrow or in several days. Normally, those who did receive a care package from home would share part of its contents with their shipmates. There was an unwritten rule about opening care packages in front of others. Recipients were obligated to share the goodies inside. Cookies, gum, licorice, beef jerky, popcorn, honey-roasted peanuts; you name it, it became public domain.

There was a "ram in the bush," though, for those who left the post office empty handed. The captain called me to his cabin and handed me a rather large box.

"Here," he said, "I want you to hand this out to the crew during chow today."

"Aye, Aye, Sir!" I acknowledged.

"And the master chief has a box of care packages I want you to distribute randomly as well."

"Yes, Sir!"

The return address on the box was from a third grade class in Pembroke Pines, Florida. There were about 100 hand-made greeting cards designed with construction paper and a lot of ingenuity and imagination. At first I was sort of skeptical about handing out children's cards to these warriors but an order was an order. So I brought the box to the Mess Deck right at the height of lunchtime, grabbed about a dozen and began with the first Sailor I saw in the chow line. I began slowly handing them out one at a time but the interest caught on like wildfire. "I will take one, Sir!" "Yeah, me too Sir!" "Send 'em down here Sir!"

It was like I was giving away fresh twenty-dollar bills.

The entire box was empty in five minutes. These guys were famished for something from home and these sweet, thoughtful, and boldly patriotic cards did the trick. These reactions got me thinking of a strategic time to hand out the care packages.

I stayed up late that night to see which sailors would be standing the Mid-Watch from 12:00 a.m. until 4:00 a.m. I went down to the Mess Deck and noticed a small group of sailors were sitting at tables eating and watching a movie on the big screen TV. They were glued, almost in a trance, to the TV set and had not noticed that I had come up behind them with the box of care packages. I opened the box, grabbed a couple of packages, and set them in front of two sailors. At first they did not know what to make of them. I grabbed two more and did the same for two others. They looked at me strangely. "Open them!" I said. The care packages transformed the grown men into young boys right before my eyes. Smiles appeared on the most unlikely faces, laughter burst forth from the toughest hearts, and gratitude towards me could not be contained. Such is the reaction to unexpected gifts from those who serve at sea.

-6-

BRIGHT STAR

Muslim not "Terrorist"

"The Egyptians are coming! The Egyptians are coming!"

These statements, adapted from our revolutionary past, best summed up the hysteria and anxiety that was spreading throughout the ship just prior to Operation BRIGHT STAR. We were heading to Egypt, a predominately Muslim country, to conduct our first exercise of the deployment. In many crewmembers' minds, Muslim meant Terrorist. Now, I knew that was not true but we could not keep the sailors and Marines from talking:

"First the COLE, now 9/11. What's next?"

"Man, they are going to blow up ship!"

"I am not sitting next to any of *them* at chow time."

Being African-American, I fully understood the pain and derision that stereotypes can produce. I also understood the pervasive apprehension and suspicion about this exercise the crew held in the wake of September 11th. There was only one thing I knew that could conquer these competing concerns, *the truth*.

Nothing dispels ignorance like the truth. Nothing deflates irrationality like the truth. Nothing enlightens perspectives during challenging circumstances like the truth. It seemed to me the crew needed a healthy dose of honest information—quickly—about the Egyptians: things like history, culture, demographics, and geo-politics. My first thought was to publish brief notes in the POD and via email. However, any such actions would first need the CO's blessing.

Operation BRIGHT STAR was a series of joint training exercises led by America and Egypt that was held bi-annually for the past two decades. It sought to strengthen ties between our nations as well as enhance our ability to reinforce our allies in the region during a conflict. Over the years, many other nations in Europe and the Middle East have participated in the exercise. Our specific task in the exercise was to perform what we did best: ship-to-shore amphibious operations that moved Marines and their machines via landing craft, assault vehicles, and helicopters.

11 October 2001

Shortly after breakfast, I was summoned by the captain to come by his cabin. I had not had a meeting in private like this since Norfolk. He wanted to get a read on crew morale. The meeting lasted less than a half hour. Afterwards, I thanked him again for his time with a short message:

From: CHAPS@SHREVEPORT
To: CO@SHREVEPORT

Subject: Thanks & prayer attached

Sir,

Thank you for the opportunity to speak with you this morning. I really appreciated our conversation. I attached the prayer I believe you were looking for. It was from last Friday, 05 October, entitled, "The Quiet before The Storm."

Very respectfully,
Chaplain Brown

Even though meetings like this one were rare, it was a good to know I had the trust and confidence of the captain.

From: CHAPS@SHREVEPORT
To: RB@HOME

Subject: Floating off of Egypt

Good Morning!

It is raining. Raining hard. We are on the edge of the world's largest desert and everyone is getting soaked! I poked my head out of the starboard side hatch to get a glimpse of sunny, clear skies but it was not to be. I figured that sunny skies were a shoe-in. How many times did it rain all day in the Mojave Desert? Anyway, we began to send the Marines ashore via LCU early this morning. They are very motivated. They are doing what they have trained to do, so all of this fits like a glove for them. Besides, they get to go ashore and at this point, anything "land" is good. They will be back in about two weeks. The offload is expected to take most of the day.

If I really thought about it, I would get a little down about being so close to Egypt and yet so far. When they briefed us on this operation months ago, I had idealistic visions of seeing the pyramids and the Sphinx. Some of the officers, who had been this way before, complained that the tour price was too high and so they did not bother to go. I would have saved one month of my split pay to go. It was that important. However, everything has changed. We live in a different world that has been restricted by the threat of terrorism. So, our trip here is just business.

I had a great conversation with the CO today. He's working really hard to get us a port visit but he is not sure when that will be. My gut tells me we are in for a long time at sea. Please continue to pray and ask the Lord to keep us strong if that is the case.

I'm holding a prayer meeting this evening to lift up the Marines and sailors involved in this operation. I mentioned that we will be out here for a couple of weeks (?) but I will let you know when we get there.

If you get a chance, give my mom a call and tell her that I am doing well. Have a blessed day!

Love,
Chaps

From: RB@HOME
To: CHAPS@SHREVEPORT

Re: Floating off of Egypt

Good Morning Chaps.

Sad news on the home front: Your aunt passed away this morning. Your cousin called to give me the news and mom called shortly after that. Please pray for the family and especially for your uncle. No details on funeral arrangements.

I will email again soon.

Love,
RB

I sat at my computer absorbing what I just read. My aunt battled against cancer for a very long time. She did well in her struggle and endured when others would have given up. *Man, I wish I could go home.* Unfortunately, there was no chance of that. On deployment, Emergency Leave was only granted for the death of an immediate family member. Besides, our current logistical situation could not support it.

My aunt had a full life experience, knowing the joy of a loving husband, three children, and as many grandchildren. She was now at home with the Lord. I wished I could be home with my family to show my support and share my grief. I knew the next best thing was a phone call to my uncle on the POTS line, a satellite connection by phone that was reserved for emergency situations like this one. *How many times have I counseled grieving sailors and offered them a private call on the POTS line?*

Now it was my turn.

I found my uncle's phone number in my address book. I did not bother to calculate what time it was back home nor did I expect him to answer the phone, understanding the circumstance. I just thought I would call and leave a message. To my surprise, he was there.

"Hello," he said.

"Hey, Uncle Ron. It's Dave. How are you?" I asked.

"Hey Dave! Man, what a surprise!" he responded. "How are you doing?"

"I am fine. I am fine. Look, Uncle Ron, I am so sorry to hear about my aunt." I said.

"Hey, thanks Dave. I really appreciate the call," he said. "Your aunt battled this for a long time but in the end it was just too strong for her."

"You know I would be right there with you and the rest of the family but I cannot make it home. I am sorry," I said.

"Hey Dave, I completely understand. Where are you?" he asked.

There was something about his question that made me pause.

"I...I am um..." *Why would he care where I was?* I had called to encourage him. *Where are you?* That question began to prick my conscience. *Where are you?* When I knew the best place to be at a time like this was home. *Where are you?* When I could not be granted Emergency Leave and there was no way to get me home even if I could. *Where are you?* Made the distance that I was from everything familiar and dear to me more tangible.

"I am...five miles...off the coast of Egypt," I answered.

"Wow! You are sure getting some great experiences. We are all really proud of you and what you are doing for the country," he said.

"Thanks. You know I would be there if I could, Uncle Ron," I said.

"Hey I understand. Just keep us in your prayers. This is not an easy time for me or your cousins," he admitted.

"I will," I said.

"Well, it was good talking to you, Dave. You be safe out there," he said.

"I will. Please tell everyone I said hi."

"Okay. Take care, now," he said.

"I will. God bless you!"

When I got back to my stateroom, I shut the hatch, turned off the light, sat still in my chair for a moment, and then whispered into the darkness:

"Where am I? Where am I?"

1758
From: CHAPS@SHREVEPORT
To: XO@SHREVEPORT

Subject: My Aunt

Sir,

Strictly FYI: My wife emailed that my aunt passed away today. She had been ill for quite a while. I have not asked her to send an AMCROSS message.

Very respectfully,
Chaplain Brown

From: XO@SHREVEPORT
To: CHAPS@SHREVEPORT

Re: My Aunt

Chaplain Brown,

My sympathies. My prayer is that your family will be brought closer to each other through her death.

R/
XO

From: CHAPS@SHREVEPORT
To: XO@SHREVEPORT

Re: My Aunt

Thank you, Sir, for your sympathies.

Chaps

The XO must have forwarded my message to the brothers from the Daily Prayer Meeting because I began to receive a flood of emails expressing sympathy for my aunt. Chief Ducass was the first:

Good evening fellow brothers in Christ! I trust you are all having a blessed day. Chaplain Brown, my friend and strong brother in Christ, received news this evening that his dear aunt passed away. On a day-to-day basis, he is busy, lifting us up, building us up, and interceding for us. So now, it is time for us to intercede for him and lift him up. He is in fine spirits and we are comforted to know that his aunt has gone to a divine place that is prepared for her. She experiences no more pain, no more agony, Praise the Lord! God bless Brothers.

Your brother in Christ,
Chief Ducass

The Marines spent all day floating and flying ashore. During these operations, I was usually touring back-and-forth between the Well Deck and the Flight Deck, fully engaged in deckplate ministry with sailors and Marines. I was so preoccupied processing my aunt's passing that I simply hunkered down in my stateroom—out of sight—with my heart and emotions numb and flat.

"TATTOO, TATTOO! LIGHTS OUT IN FIVE MINUTES! STAND BY FOR THE EVENING PRAYER."

The Ship Rests

Let us pray.

Gracious Lord, there is a silence about the decks this evening that has not been experienced in several weeks. It is as if the ship has exhaled a gasp of relief after a long, arduous day at sea. Within hours SHREVEPORT has changed her complexion but in doing so has once again fulfilled her sole purpose.

The ship begins to rest, not with a snoring slumber but a vigilant hush, its only signature being the wake of the screws as she steams a nautical night box.

Lord, we offer a prayer of protection for our teammates gone ashore. May their training be productive and safe in cooperation and conjunction with the other land forces. We offer a similar prayer for our crew. May our lives be protected by your presence among us. We offer a joint petition that covers all of our loved ones. Stand by and strengthen them with your mighty hand.

Whatever our hands find to do, let us do it with peace in our hearts, all of our strength, and to the best of our ability.

All this we ask in your Holy Name.

Amen.

PREPPING FOR OUR GUESTS
The burden of the host

13 October 2001

I had a few ideas about several topics I wanted to cover in my "Honest Information Campaign" to the crew. Before I could gather them all to brief the CO, the XO delivered a message from the CO that I did not expect. All the mounting hysteria and anxiety about the arrival of the Egyptians had reached the CO and prompted him to consider canceling the Evening Prayer at Sea. He was concerned that the Egyptians might find my prayers religiously offensive. Canceling the prayer would be the logical, quick-and-easy solution. I was 110 percent opposed to this but what could I do? The Evening Prayer at Sea was always conducted at the commanding officer's discretion. It was completely his decision.

"The CO has pretty much made up his mind on this one," the XO told me. "Unless you can convince him otherwise, be prepared not to do the Evening Prayer while the Egyptians are onboard the ship."

After this notification, I headed for my stateroom, shut the hatch and sat down for a moment of silent prayer with the Lord. He already knew what I was going to ask but asked Him anyway:

Lord, grant me the words to persuade the CO to keep the Evening Prayer in place. The prayer is your moment to reach the crew. Please do not let fear or anxieties block it from taking place. In Jesus' name, I pray. Amen.

From: CHAPS@SHREVEPORT
To: CO@SHREVEPORT

Cc: XO@SHREVEPORT

Subject: POD Notes and Pastoral Care Plan for our "Guests"

Sir,

Here is the tentative plan for the POD Notes and Pastoral Care Plan for our guests, the Egyptians:

POD Notes (subjects):

- 14 October: Overview of the country: General travelogue information, facts and figures
- 15 October: Summary of Islamic faith–A "nuts and bolts" familiarization
- 16 October: Culture – Practices, trends, and taboos
- 17 October: Geo-Political Status – Allied, moderate Arab state with some radical factions
- 18 October: Military (Navy) – How they "stack up" and the regional role they play

These five notes can be rerun or canceled upon the arrival of our guests.

Pastoral Care Concerns:

I will treat the Egyptians as I would any guests to our ship: with courtesy, compassion, and the right to reserve suspicion only when warranted. In Christian terms, I will be "as wise as a serpent but as gentle as a dove."

I respectfully recommend that we continue to offer the Evening Prayer at Sea. Here are several reasons why: First, it is the right thing to do not only for tradition's sake but also for the way that prayer upholds and sustains this vessel and the crew. The welds, rivets, angle irons, and frame of the ship are more or less hanging in there after thirty-one years of wear and tear. Nothing else can completely cover the spirit, morale, hope, and faith of the crew—all at the same time—as the instance of the Evening Prayer. Besides, it is something the crew expects at the end of the evening. Second, I can amend the prayer to remove certain idiomatic expressions that might be offensive or, at the very least, misunderstood. Third, we are Americans. Our laws provide for the free exercise of religion and this would be a perfect opportunity to show we can accommodate diversity in faith in peace, even agree to disagree without being disagreeable. Lastly, our guests must abide by the rules of the house. We have implemented movement restrictions about the ship and briefed a Force Protection Plan that we fully intend to enact and expect our guests to abide. They may agree or disagree but these are the house rules. Again, I recommend we keep the Evening Prayer as part of that package.

Regarding specifics on Islamic worship, we will do our best to accommodate their needs. We can make the First Class Mess available as a space to conduct worship and their daily prayers. Also, 19 October 2001 is the beginning of Ramadan, a thirty-day period of fasting and prayer.

As always, I am at your service and available to provide advice at your discretion.

Very respectfully,
Chaplain Brown

From: CO@SHREVEPORT
To: CHAPS@SHREVEPORT
Cc: XO@SHREVEPORT

Re: POD Notes and Pastoral Care Plan for our "Guests"

Okay. Good job. You appear to have covered all the bases.

Concur with your recommendation to continue the evening prayer. Just give the evening prayer as you normally do, being only slightly sensitive to the presence of our non-Christian guests.

I had not thought about their requirement for daily prayer, although I should have. There may be as many as 120 of them, so the First Class Mess may be a little tight. An alternative may be the Signal Bridge at the top of the ship.

Incorporate your plan, as modified above, into the larger embark plan. Again, good work.

R/
CO

Thank you, Lord!

I was very relieved by the CO's response. Conducting the Evening Prayer at Sea would send a clear signal to our guests:

Matters of faith matter to us

Mid-Morning

"FLIGHT QUARTERS, FLIGHT QUARTERS! ALL HANDS MAN YOUR FLIGHT QUARTERS STATIONS! WEAR NO COVERS TOPSIDE, THROW NO ARTICLES OVER THE SIDE. ALL HANDS NOT INVOLVED WITH FLIGHT QUARTERS STAND CLEAR OF THE FLIGHT DECK, HANGAR BAY, AND THE WEATHER DECKS!"

I always enjoyed receiving notes of encouragement from pastors or church members back home. One such message met me this morning at the top of my email queue. It was from a congregant at Bethel AME Church in Baton Rouge, Louisiana.

From: VSMITH@HOME
To: CHAPS@SHREVEPORT

Subject: Encouragement for our AME Chaplains

Dear Chaplains:

At the urging of Chaplain Sydnor and our pastor, the Bethel Baton Rouge family thanks you for your courage and we would like to offer these words of encouragement and prayer as you begin your deployment ministry.

With your permission, I would like to share your email address with our congregation, particularly our Youth Bible Study so they may be a source of prayer and strength for you all during these difficult days. Until then, "Don't let adversity get you down except on your knees."

Amen.

Ms. Valerie Smith

From: CHAPS@SHREVEPORT
To: VSMITH@HOME

Re: Encouragement for our AME Chaplains

Dear Ms. Smith,

I am Chaplain David Brown, the President of the AME Chaplain's Association. I am currently in the thick of things on deployment. How wonderful and encouraging it is to know that our home folk are keeping my colleagues and I lifted high in prayer! The support we have received thus far has been tremendous and with messages like yours, it only seems to be growing. Praise the Lord for those like you who believe in a Sovereign God and the overcoming power of prayer!

We will do our best to keep the church updated with as much information as we are allowed to transmit. Please know we are doing well, serving the Lord, and representing our denomination to the best of our abilities.

May the Lord bless you always!

Yours in Christ,

David R. Brown
Lieutenant, U.S. Navy
Chaplain Corps

Early Afternoon

With the Marines ashore, the ship was quiet and remained that way until the Egyptians arrived about a week later. My days, though, were filled with so many "Jabez" opportunities I knew that I could not manage them on my own strength. I was in the White Library gathering information for the POD notes for several days.

We were expecting a mail drop later that afternoon, perhaps as much as five thousand to six thousand pounds. I was hoping that one to two pounds of it would be something from home. My mother wrote a short note letting me know that she had received the letter I sent to her from Spain just three days after I sent it. That was super-fast!

The Honest Information Campaign would begin tomorrow. When the POD was read at morning quarters, the entire crew would hear the information I put together. I hoped it would have a positive effect on the crew's understanding about our impending guests.

"THE SHIP IS AT FLIGHT QUARTERS! ALL HANDS NOT INVOLVED WITH FLIGHT QUARTERS STAND CLEAR OF THE FLIGHT DECK, THE HANGAR BAY, AND THE WEATHER DECKS."

God our Protector

Let us pray.

"Whoever goes to the Lord for safety, whoever remains under the protection of the Almighty, can say to him, 'You are my defender and protector. You are my God; in you I trust.'"[2]

Gracious Lord, our confidence is stirred tonight by the fact that you are our defender and protector. Confidence in today's world is a rare commodity; once purchased is seldom sold even to the highest bidder. Those who seek you receive it and are blessed by the exchange you offer:

Your peace for our anxiety
Your assurance for our apprehension
Faith for our doubt
Love for our apathy

Lord, prompt us to place our trust in you. Then, we will experience a confidence—not in ourselves but in you that can never be shaken.

In your Strong Name we pray,

Amen

14 October

"REVEILLE, REVEILLE! ALL HANDS HEAVE OUT! BREAKFAST FOR THE CREW!

The email I received from Ms. Smith from Baton Rouge, Louisiana was an icebreaker for my fellow deployed colleagues. We began talking to each other. Our cross-communication brought mutual encouragement but also served to solidify that God had placed us out here, forward deployed to

---

[2] Adapted from reading Psalm 91:1-2

minister to the spiritual needs of our personnel. Chaplain Harold Ashford, an Air Force Chaplain stationed in Turkey, was the first message of the day.

From: HASHFORD@IZMIR
To: CHAPS@SHREVEPORT

Subject: A New Day

Hi Chaplain Brown!

Thanks for all you are doing to keep us on track in spite of the current situation. I am in Izmir and we are with you and many others on the tip of the spear. So I say to you "Go Navy and US Forces!"

It gets interesting at times around here. We have had to ask ourselves some hard questions about our faith. Questions about what we really believe about God and how we express faith to those we serve. As I look back, I am glad that we were put on the spot following September 11th. It made me reconfirm what I believe and why I believe and in whom I believe.

This is just a quick note to say, "Hello" and thanks for being faithful to your duties as our AME Chaplain's Association President and the sacred pastoral work you are performing in the Navy. God bless and keep you in the Good Work!

I am reading a great book you might be interested in reading. It is *The Prayer of Jabez*. What a book filled with powerful insight for those of us who walk by faith! Got to go for now.

Chaplain Ashford

From: CHAPS@SHREVEPORT
To: HASHFORD@IZMIR

Re: A New Day

Chaplain Ashford,

I too am a Jabez fan and practitioner. I discovered this book about seven months ago and it has literally changed my life and ministry. I pray that the Lord would continue to bless you indeed in all that you do for Him.

Yours in Christ,
Chaplain Brown

The next message was from Chaplain Jennings Harrison aboard the USS KITTY HAWK, which was disseminated by Chaplain Sydnor throughout the Church:

Thank you for your prayers. The stress out here is unreal and the overseas deployment environment is something else! It seems that individuals have a tendency to vent their frustrations on those of the Cloth. However, I am continuing to stand in the midst of this adversity. Our Air Wing community needs your prayers as well as all those who find themselves in harm's way. I truly appreciate my AME family.

Blessings and Peace,
Chaplain Jennings Harrison

Mid-Afternoon
From: RB@HOME
To: CHAPS@SHREVEPORT

Subject: Can you send flowers?

Hey! Just wanted to know what your plan was for sending flowers for my Aunt. Did you want to send them or would you like me to do it? I can send either a bouquet or a fruit basket to your uncle's house but please let me know soon. Thanks!

RB

From: CHAPS@SHREVEPORT
To: RB@HOME

Re: Can you send flowers?

Go ahead and order the flowers online. It will be much quicker if you do it.

I got my first piece of mail last night from Mom. She sent it on 05 October almost ten days earlier. We are getting another mail drop today and tomorrow.

I am still doing well out here. I am getting busy! A lot of research is going into the composition of the POD notes about Egypt.

Take care,
Chaps

"TATTOO, TATTOO! LIGHTS OUT IN FIVE MINUTES! STAND BY FOR THE EVENING PRAYER."

Audible Stillness

"Be still and know that I am God; I will be exalted among the nations, exalted in all the earth."[3]

Sovereign God, sometimes it is not easy to keep our composure when uncertainty lowers our tolerance for fear. Mix in routine and unavoidable fatigue and it creates a perfect recipe for being on edge.

Before anxieties flare or words become glowing sparks tossed at puddles of gasoline, we ought to consider this thought:

---

[3] Psalm 46:10

Do we dare be still enough to hear your voice? To actually remain silent long enough for you to get a word, a consonant or a vowel into our soul? Silence so still it makes a pin-drop conspicuous, so quiet that our own pulse seems boisterous.

O God, impress upon us our need to create a space for audible stillness in our hearts, a place just big enough for two so that when you speak we can hear you "LIMA CHARLIE" ("Loud" and "Clear"). When we speak, your patience to listen extends to everything you already know we want to say.

"Be still and know that I am God; I will be exalted among the nations, exalted in all the earth."

Amen.

15 October
0648

From: RB@HOME
To: CHAPS@SHREVEPORT

Re: Can you send flowers?

Hey! I checked online and they have a beautiful bouquet in a vase for a very reasonable price. They also have a fruit basket for just slightly higher. Should I go with one of these or something else? Please respond ASAP so that I can move on this today.

RB

From: CHAPS@SHREVEPORT

To: RB@HOME

Re: Can you send flowers?

Please send the bouquet. I am sure they are beautiful and will be appreciated by the family.

It looks like I have a full day of research and writing ahead of me today. I am starting to feel like a Public Affairs Officer. Whew!

More to follow...I have to catch up with Derby later for PT.

Love,
Chaps

Late Evening
From: RB@HOME
To: CHAPS@SHREVEPORT

Re: Can you send flowers?

Mission accomplished! The flowers will be delivered on Tuesday. Please pray for safe travel to and from Richmond. We will be going up on Tuesday and returning on Wednesday. Also, please pray for my strength. I am wearing down trying to keep up with our very active son. There are many times I cannot finish dinner, read the paper, or type an email without stopping to give him the attention he deserves. All of this is just so much easier when you are around to help. Please pray for us. We need it and I definitely need it. Talk to you soon.

Love,
RB

My heart went out to my wife on this one but I did not want to respond with a knee-jerk response. In spite of how I felt, I had to sleep on this and respond in the morning. Besides, it was past 2100 and I had to focus on preparing for the Evening Prayer.

Lord, let me respond well to the needs of my wife. Guide my heart and my hands in the morning to send a message that blesses and encourages her heart. Amen.

Rightful Praise

"It is good to give thanks to the Lord and to praise your name, O Most High."(Psalm 92:1)

O Lord, it should not be a difficult thing,
To give you praise and let our heart sing.

If we just take a moment to think it through,
Our lives have been blessed all because of you.

Our praises should flow like whitewater breakers,
And drift into the ears of our Almighty Maker.

Each morning is a new chance to be led through the day,
Your abundant grace clearing a path along the way.

You keep all our loved ones under your special care
How well you watch after them, though we're not even there.

For who you are and all that you've done,
We give you praise, O Righteous, Holy One.

"It is good to give thanks to the Lord and to praise your name, O Most High."

Amen.

16 October
Morning Quarters

I showed up to Quarters this morning to get a sense of how the POD notes were being received by the crew. Today's write-up was about Egyptian culture. The petty officer read the notes in a matter-of-fact manner and was received the same way by the sailors. *Man, I put some work, some research into this. Wow!* For some reason, I had this idealistic notion that my hard work would have some immediate and transformational effect on its audience. It seemed that most of the sailors were barely awake, which I now feared had been the case all week throughout the ship. Knowing this, it was going to be harder to stay motivated to keep researching and writing for the next two days. However, an order was an order.

0750
Re: Can you send flowers?

Gracious Lord,

I pray for your blessing of strength to be upon my wife as she watches over and raises our son. Let her know that this task is far too great for her own strength. Let her rely totally on your strength alone. Let her be refreshed and blessed by the power you alone can provide

Continue to grow our son in every aspect and every way. Bless him with intelligence, health, and peace of mind; prepare him for every good thing you have for him in your time and for your glory.

Strengthen us as a couple. It is not easy to take on the sacrifice of being apart from each other. You have been faithful to us and have blessed us in so many ways. Great is your faithfulness!

Bless us, Lord! Bless us, indeed! Stand by my wife and son as they head to Richmond. Keep them safe from all hurt, harm, and danger. Let them join with the rest of the family as they celebrate the life of my dear aunt. Surround them all with your comfort as they cope with her loss.

I pray this in Jesus name, Amen.

Flowers sent.

Mid-Morning
From: BISHOPHENNING@AMEC
To: CHAPS@SHREVEPORT

Subject: Re: NEWS FROM A DEPLOYED NAVY CHAPLAIN

(Chaplain Brown) We praise God for your safe arrival and for your great spirit as you prepare to lead military members on a very special spiritual journey. Please know that I, as well as a great host of others, am praying for you and all our chaplains.

Bishop Henning

Another note of encouragement from my church: this time it was from Bishop C. Garnett Henning, who presided over our 19th Episcopal District in South Africa.

"*DAILY PRAYER MEETING WILL BE HELD IN SACC AT 1230.*"

Back to the library this afternoon to do more research for tomorrow's POD notes. In the midst of my reading, I began to second-guess my efforts, wondering if any of this was making a difference. I knew that the ugly comments and attitudes towards our guests had to stop. In less than seventy-two hours, the Egyptians would be aboard the ship. Then what? Tensions were still high and with one wrong word or gesture—Whew! The last thing we needed was an incident aboard the ship. Was the Arabic/English language barrier between them and our crew enough to keep the peace? I simply did not know.

"*SWEEPERS! SWEEPERS! MAN YOUR BROOMS! GIVE THE SHIP A GOOD SWEEP-DOWN BOTH FORWARD AND AFT. SWEEP-DOWN ALL LADDERWELLS, LADDERBACKS, AND PASSAGEWAYS! HOLD ALL TRASH AND GARBAGE ON STATION!*"

Help

Gracious Lord, we need your help tonight. The things we need and so desire are out of our reach. There is a Rolodex filled with so many secret wishes that we would almost invite you to take a pick: fatigue, peace of mind, healing, more joy, worry, fighting boredom, escaping loneliness, et cetera and so forth. We seek a remedy for these ailments.

If it could be purchased, we would own it.
If it could be stored, we would stockpile it.
If it could be made, we would have the patent.
If it could be done on our own, we would not bother you at all.

But it can't—and that is not our cue to despair. Rather, we ought to remember that our extremity is your opportunity to act. Your response to our predicament is a rhetorical one:

"Is there anything too hard for the Lord?"

O Lord, fill in the gaps and bridge the chasms that foster discouragement, disillusionment, or doubt. Do your divine work of looking past our faults and seeing our needs. Meet them in a way we would immediately recognize as your abundant provision.

We ask this in your Holy Name,

Amen.

-8-

UNDERWAY BIRTHDAY
It's the thought that counts

17 October 2001

"REVEILLE, REVEILLE! ALL HANDS HEAVE OUT!
BREAKFAST FOR THE CREW!"

0857
From: GB@HOME (Apple iCards)
To: CHAPS@SHREVEPORT

Subject: G Brown has sent you an Apple iCard

HAPPY BIRTHDAY CHAPS!

Love, GB

My youngest brother sent me an electronic birthday card today. I opened
the link and the above message appeared with a simple picture of a group
of lit candles on a birthday cake.

From: CHAPS@SHREVEPORT
To: GB@HOME (Apple iCards)

Re: G Brown has sent you an Apple iCard

Thank you Brown family!!!!! :-)

Love,
Chaps

Throughout the day, sailors all over the ship came up to me and wished me a "Happy Birthday." It seems word got out—somehow—that today was my day. It felt good.

From: CHAPS@SHREVEPORT
To: RB@HOME

Subject: Having a great B'day!

Hey!

I am having a great birthday today! The workload is lifting and the mail keeps coming. We have another drop today so I will keep my eyes peeled :-) I know on the family front that it is a sad day too. We lifted up everyone in our entire family before the Lord at the Daily Prayer Meeting. There are some strong brothers in the Lord who know how to get a prayer through. Please let me know how everything goes.

I love you very much. I thank God every day that I am married to you and we have such a wonderful son.

Love,
Chaps

1830

Wardroom

When I entered the Wardroom, my fellow officers had orchestrated a surprise. About six or seven of them burst out into the *Happy Birthday* song just after I shut the hatch. I stood there in the center of the room, grinning and taking in their slightly out-of-tune rendition of the song. When it was over, applause and congratulations followed.

"Come on over here, Chaps. We've got a special seat for you," said one of the officers. It was "special" indeed: a solitary white plate with a box of Dots gumdrops and a Snickers Bar with one single candle stuck in the middle of it. I appreciated the sentiment.

"How many years, Chaps?" asked one officer sitting across from me.

"Uh, Thirty-seven," I said.

"Thirty-seven? Whoa, Chaps! You are getting up there," he said.

"Yeah, Chaps. You are an old man now. You are kissing forty!" said the officer seated next to him.

"Thirty-seven is old? Really?" I responded in disbelief.

I picked up the box of Dots, raised it, gave it a shake and said, "Hey, thanks everybody. I really appreciate the thought."

"No problem, Chaps."

"Happy Birthday Chaps!"

I took my gift plate to the mess line to get dinner all the while conceding that thirty-seven was old when I considered that over 80 percent of the crew was between the ages of eighteen to twenty-four years old. Most of the officers were around twenty-five.

From: GB@HOME (Apple iCards)
To: CHAPS@SHREVEPORT

Re: G Brown has sent you an Apple iCard

Hey Chaps!

We just got in from the funeral—what a day! There was a really bad accident on 95 North. It took us four hours to travel the fifty miles from Richmond to Fredericksburg. Grueling! Luckily, everyone hung in there well, even the small children.

We saw your family today. Your wife looks great and your son was very playful with his cousins at Uncle Ron's house.

It is about midnight so I am going to sign off. Chaps, be blessed and keep the faith. God is on his throne, Jesus is seated next him, and the Holy Spirit abides within us.

Greater is he within us than he that is in the world.

Take care,
GB

From: RB@HOME
To: CHAPS@SHREVEPORT

Re: Having a great B'day !

HAPPY BIRTHDAY TO YOU! HAPPY BIRTHDAY TO YOU! HAPPY BIRTHDAY DEAR C-H-A-P-S, HAPPY BIRTHDAY TO YOU—AND MANY MORE!

I realize that by the time you get this you will be thirty-seven plus one day older. I hope it was a good one. It is definitely a first for you spending your birthday at sea.

Just wanted to give you a brief update of our day: I met your cousin Sylvia last night at the wake. Your aunt looked beautiful and at peace. There were many family friends present. The service was over by 8:00 p.m.

I decided to stay at Mom's another night so I could pay a visit to your uncle. The funeral service was a beautiful and wonderful celebration of life. There was no eulogy but a number of responsive prayers, singing, and communion was served. The service lasted an hour and the internment was in northern Virginia. I decided not to go as I thought the trip would be too long for our son. I called your uncle's house around 3:30 to see if the family returned. I spoke to Sylvia, who was helping out at the house. She said there was a big traffic backup on 95 South due to an earlier accident and the procession had to take a detour. The family did not get home until 7:00 p.m.

We decided to visit your uncle's house at 8:00 p.m. Our son fussed for about twenty minutes because he was Mr. Tired Man. He had just fallen asleep in the car on the way over there and I had to wake him up to go into the house. He was crying. So we walked around the house and he met up with his cousin, who is about the same age. He was playing with his hair and nose and interacting with him. He did the same with another same-age cousin, touching her hair and nose. Then, three other cousins who are slightly older began interacting with him too. He had a great time! Unfortunately, he got tired and fussy again and I hoped he would have slept until we got back to Mom's house. As soon as I stepped outside the house, he got a second burst of energy and he is up and kicking even as I type this close to midnight.

Just wanted to say we are doing well. I should be back home around midday on Thursday. Continue to keep us in your prayers.

Love,
RB

"TATTOO, TATTOO! LIGHTS OUT IN FIVE MINUTES! STAND BY FOR THE EVENING PRAYER."

Strength Reinforced

Gracious Lord, we thank you for the strength you provide: the strength that reinforces our weary minds and bodies.

New strength:
Strength reinforced for the long haul of marking time

We have got just about a month down, nearly thirty days under our belts. It got that way by taking it one day at a time. Forgetting about the calendar to the point where someone needed to remind us what day it was, which perhaps is the best way to do time at sea.

New Strength:
Strength reinforced for the long hours spent standing Watch.

To be able to look past its regimen and routine and understand its purpose;
to be greeted by our Watch relief, whose fresh energy is set to give our sagging
eyelids and contagious yawning a welcome break, to hit the rack and savor
the sweetness of sleep.

New Strength:
Strength reinforced for the long journey taken with you.

Lord, before we become distracted or we wander away or we forget that you
are the source of our strength and the strength of our life, strengthen us this
evening for the challenges of tomorrow by your eternal power.

This we pray in your Mighty Name,

Amen.

-9-

EMINENT ARRIVAL
Twenty-four hours and counting

18 October 2001
0846

THANK YOU, THANK YOU, THANK YOU for the great birthday
wish! I can almost hear your voice singing that tune :-)
Thanks for the update on the funeral. I am glad my aunt looked like she was
at peace. Episcopalians usually do not have long services so I was not surprised when you told me the entire service lasted only an hour. I thought you
had met Sylvia, though, at some point when we used to live in Richmond.
She is really nice and she does not live far from Mom and Dad.
Sounds like our son had his own playgroup among his cousins. He will do
very well with other kids because he is naturally a sociable kid. It was pleasing
to hear about his interactions. It reminded me of how it was when I grew up
with my cousins, who were also around my age.

Well, tomorrow is the thirty-day point in the deployment. Do you think
it is going by fast or is it just going? Some days it feels like it is zipping by
and then it will lag but pick up again. If we can get over the hump of our
current exercise we will feel a sense of relief. There is a rumor of a port visit

in our future but I will keep you updated as to whether or not something materializes.

My love and my heart are always with you. I will talk to you again soon. Have a safe and blessed trip back home.

Love,
Chaps

Negotiations with the Navy Chaplain Corps Detailer

There is a saying in the Navy, "The detailer chooses your first duty station and your spouse chooses the rest." Actually, the chaplain corps detailer was the officer who was responsible for every assignment for chaplains to specific duty stations throughout the Navy. However, for married chaplains, all negotiations with orders began at home. Before I left, my wife and I discussed places where we would like to be stationed. Puerto Rico, Spain, San Diego, Jacksonville—just take your pick, or so it seemed. These choices were available but we decided to ask for a more practical one—Naval Station Norfolk. If we could be assigned there, it would guarantee three years of shore duty, which would be a welcome break from the sea.

Negotiations with the detailer for a Sailor's next set of orders could take place within one year of the end of their tour also known as the rotation date. I was within that window so I sent an email to the detailer with six duty preferences and he responded:

1. Naval Station in Norfolk, Virginia
2. Naval Station in Roosevelt Roads, Puerto Rico
3. Naval Station in Pascagoula, Mississippi

I asked him to put me down for Norfolk. This was a win/win choice, saving the Navy the cost of moving my family and allowing me to come home every night due to shore duty. I was pleased.

"DAILY PRAYER MEETING WILL BE HELD IN SACC AT 1230."

We broke from our pattern of "Gator Squares" just offshore to head out to the open ocean to conduct an UNREP. Taking on tens-of-thousands of gallons of diesel fuel and JP-8 aviation fuel as well as several tons of fresh fruit and vegetables, perishable and non-perishable stores was an all-hands evolution. To get this job done, our ship would be spending several hours tethered, sailing alongside a supply ship from Military Sealift Command.

I broke away from observing the UNREP to head back to the library to complete my last round of research and writing for the POD. I can say that I learned a few things that I did not know about Egypt through this task. For me, the real proof in the pudding would be actually meeting them in-person. In my mind, nothing would compare to firsthand experience of engaging our joint exercise partners during chow time, at meetings, and all throughout the ship. It would all start in less than twenty-four hours.

From: JAB@HOME
To: CHAPS@SHREVEPORT

Subject: Happy Birthday Brother – from JAB

Hello! JAB has just sent you a greeting card from Cobaltmountain.com You can pick up your personal message here:

http://www3.cobaltmountain.com.ca/boxb3.html

Your card will be available for the next 90 days. This service is 100% FREE! :) Have a good day and have fun!

Belated but greatly appreciated (Thanks Bro!)

"OPS/INTEL BRIEF, WARDROOM."

A "Standard Bell" (fifteen knots) was ordered for our transit back to the coast of Egypt. During our transit, the OPS/INTEL Brief was held in the Wardroom. The focus was on the entire ship's preparation for the arrival of

Egyptian soldiers. Force Protection took center stage as each presenter briefed the captain on the security measures that would be in place prior to their arrival.

The Egyptians would journey out to the ship using Zodiac speedboats and Combat Rubber Raiding Craft or CRRCs (pronounced "Cricks"). These boats were made of specially fabricated inflatable rubber and were used by Special Forces, like Navy SEALs, for raids, reconnaissance, etc. They were going to send about a dozen in several series out to us and embark the ship through the Well Deck. Once aboard, the Egyptian soldiers would be sent through several stations—Security, Admin, Medical, berthing—then be given a "Welcome" by the captain and a series of orientation briefs by the department heads with the help of an interpreter.

The captain closed the brief by re-emphasizing the importance of treating our guests really well; they were our partners in this exercise and he expected the entire crew to be professional.

2155

Cooperation

Gracious Lord, we thank you for the spirit of cooperation that was displayed aboard the ship throughout the day. While taking on fuel and striking down stores, the ship was fully re-supplied as sailors literally worked hand-in-hand to get the job done.

Lord, is it enough to mention that the crew was just doing their duty? Perhaps, but there is something that should always impress us about willing service: No sacrifice is ever so small that it should be overlooked.

What the crew accomplished today is nothing short of keeping the ship afloat. Of course, the ship's engineering, watertight integrity, and salt-water buoyancy all played a part. Most importantly it is people, our most valuable asset that keeps the ship running smoothly above the surface.

Thank you, Lord, for every helping hand, every willing heart, and every second of service and sacrifice we have experienced today.

All this we pray in your Merciful Name,

Amen.

"TAPS, TAPS, LIGHTS OUT! ALL HANDS TURN TO YOUR BUNKS. MAINTAIN SILENCE ABOUT THE DECKS. TAPS!"

-10-

THE EGYPTIANS ARE HERE

There's nothing to fear

19 October

0530

"SET CONDITION 1-ALPHA FOR WELL DECK OPERATIONS!
SET CONDITION 1-ALPHA FOR WELL DECK OPERATIONS!"

After breakfast, I headed straight for the Well Deck to observe the set up for the arrival of the Egyptians. The Stern Gate had been lowered and the ship ballasted down to flood the Well Deck to the depth of seven feet, more than enough seawater to allow the Egyptian CRRCs to come aboard the ship. The boatswain mates from Deck Department were already in the Well Deck anticipating the arrival of the CRRCs. They were wearing the standard personal protective gear for Well Deck Ops: blue hard-hats, float-coat vests, and old-worn boots—the kind they did not mind getting wet. They would be responsible for assisting with the safe embarkation of the Egyptian soldiers and the proper mooring and stowing of their CRRCs.

Boatswain Mates huddle in the Well Deck

The security force was there too, heavily armed with M-16 rifles, bulletproof vests with extra magazine clips on each side, black ball caps, and leather gloves. Six of them had already taken positions—three on each side—of the upper walkways of the Well Deck. This vantage point gave them the perfect high-ground position from which to discharge their weapons, should it be necessary to do so. Each check-in station had an interpreter as well as the appropriate personnel, and a member of the security force on Watch directly behind them.

The first series of CRRCs came into view of the open Well Deck. The first one to approach had eight Egyptian soldiers, four seated on each side, with a coxswain in the middle steering the craft. When the CRRC was within twenty yards, the soldiers pulled out oars and paddled the boat the rest of the way into the ship. The boatswain mates, who secured the vessel first with their hands and then with ropes, were the first to meet them. As soon as they debarked the boat, a member of the security force directed them over to the first check-in station, which was manned by another member of the force holding a hand-held metal detector. One-by-one, each soldier headed over to the station and placed their weapons down on the table, took off their float coats, and stood straight with arms extended so the Sailor with the metal detector could pass it over them—from head–to-toe, front and back. The soldiers wore a desert camouflage patterned uniform and black boots and most of them were my skin tone or slightly lighter in complexion.

The next several CRRCs followed the pattern: arrival at the Stern Gate, mooring in the Well Deck, and debarking of soldiers. The Well Deck was filled with commotion—their soldiers and our sailors beginning their collaborative work. They slowly made their way from one check-in station to the next and it seemed most either understood or spoke some English. The captain was now on hand with the XO to observe the evolution as well as be present for the arrival of their commander-of-troops. He was also slated to be the first to address the Egyptians once they all arrived.

With all the soldiers aboard, it was time to kick-off the welcome. There was a PA system set up with a hand-held microphone and two speakers that could project over the working noise within the Well Deck. The soldiers were summoned to make a semi-circle around the captain who spoke and then handed the microphone to the interpreter, who handed it back to the captain so he could continue his remarks. After a few sentences, one could see the need for two microphones instead of one. It was bit awkward and I began to wonder, judging by the soldiers' body language, how much of this was sticking.

The captain wrapped up his comments by handing off the microphone to us, his department heads, so that we could have the opportunity to introduce ourselves to the soldiers. Starting with the XO, the microphone shuffle began; department head spoke, interpreter followed. My turn was coming up and I had already made up in my mind that I would be brief, just mentioning only my name and position. Then the Holy Spirit spoke to me and said:

Use the Arabic You Know to Speak to Them

I was startled! I did not know much Arabic at all. Fortunately, I did not have any time to think about it because it was my turn to address the soldiers. I moved to the center of the circle, took hold of the microphone with my right hand while slightly raising my left, and said, *"A salaam alaikum"* ("Peace be upon you").

"Wa-alaikum salaam!" ("And unto you, peace"), was the soldiers' response in near-unison.

Immediately I sensed that I had their attention. So I continued, now pointing to myself, *"Da-woud, Da-woud,"* ("David, David" or "My name is David"*)*

"Dawoud!" they responded, some with smiles and heads nodding.

"Chaplain *Dawoud,* I said in conclusion.

"Dawoud!" they responded again.

I turned over the microphone to the interpreter and thought, *Wow! A connection.*

"Hey, Chaps, looks like you've got them eating out of your hand," whispered one of my fellow officers.

"Yeah, I guess so," I said.

It felt good to break through. *Now what? How did God want me to use this connection?*

"DINNER FOR THE CREW!"

Out of curiosity, I ventured down to the Mess Deck to see how the sailors and soldiers were faring. The Mess Deck Master-At-Arms had a few extra sailors on watch, who were positioned at each corner of the Mess Deck to increase security. *What do you know?* The soldiers and sailors were in the same chow lines, using the same soda fountains, and picked fruits and fresh vegetables from the same salad station. They had even integrated tables— groups of two to three at each one—and were, unremarkably, getting along and eating dinner. The mere presence of the soldiers among the crew seemed to be working far better than my POD notes ever could. *What in the world was all the hype and hysteria about? The Egyptians are here...the Egyptians are here. Huh! There is nothing to fear, the Egyptians are here.*

"TATTOO, TATTOO! LIGHTS OUT IN FIVE MINUTES! STAND BY FOR THE EVENING PRAYER."

Guests

*Most merciful and benevolent God, we thank you for giving us another
blessed day at sea. Thank you also for the safe arrival of our guests, members
of the Egyptian military.*

*Continue to show your mercy as we live and train together over the next
four days. Give us the will to learn from each other and to expand our
understanding so that we may grow together as allies.*

Grant us rest this evening and strength to stand the Watch.

In your Merciful Name we pray,

Amen.

20 October
Mid-Morning

"NOW SET OPSECON ONE! NOW SET OPSECON ONE! MAKE ALL REPORTS TO RADIO AT EXTENSION 7745."

Email was shut down but I could not figure out why. Everyone knew
we were in Egypt and we were executing BRIGHT STAR. I hoped there
was not an accident involving casualties with sailors or Marines. I headed
up to the Pilot House to see what the Officer-of-the-Deck knew. It turned
out that one of our ships, the WHIDBEY ISLAND, had temporarily run
aground. They came too close to the shore and hit an uncharted sandbar.
All the navigation charts show the water's depth to have been more than
sufficient to support the draft of the ship. However, the sandbar, considered
a tidal anomaly, was big enough to trap the ship in the shallows and create
some damage. The Officer-of-the-Deck believed this incident was not significant enough for someone to get fired.

SHREVEPORT had its own record of grounding which it was trying
to escape. Back in February 2000, the ship ran aground three times during a
northbound transit of the Suez Canal. The damage caused was so significant

that it could not make the journey home to Norfolk but was diverted to a dry dock in Haifa, Israel to be repaired. I remember hearing about this while I was still stationed at the Naval Training Center in Great Lakes, Illinois. I had orders in hand to report to the ship and all I could think of was what kind of morale issues I was going to inherit once I reported. Ship driving was an inherently dangerous and unforgiving profession.

"DAILY PRAYER MEETING WILL BE HELD IN SACC AT 1230."

From: CHAPS@SHREVEPORT
To: RB@HOME

Subject: Good Day!

Hey!

We just heard rumors of a port visit as soon as we are done here in Egypt. The entire crew is anxious to get on dry land once again and enjoy some liberty. I will be sure to send plenty of souvenirs. I have four rolls of film left that I purchased in Rota so I will take lots of pictures.

Have the leaves changed colors yet? If so, take a few digital shots if you get the chance. From what I can see of the shoreline, all the vegetation is still green here.

Love,
Chaps

From: RB@HOME
To: CHAPS@SHREVEPORT

Re: Good Day!

I should have taken some digitals in Richmond. The leaves were at their peak and were beautiful. I have not seen so much of that here, seeing that the pine trees dominate the landscape. I will see if I can get Mom to take a picture with her camera and send it to me so I can send it to you.

That's all for now. I hope you do get to dry land soon. You deserve a break. Take care and God bless you!

Love,
RB

I missed the fall. It was the first one that I have ever missed in my entire life. Eventually, Thanksgiving and Christmas would follow suit. Sometimes it seemed like there was only one season on a shipboard deployment—underway.

"NOW SET OPSECON NORMAL! NOW SET OPSECON NORMAL! MAKE ALL REPORTS TO RADIO AT EXTENSION 7745."

Early Evening

Tonight commenced the series of generic prayers that I proposed to the captain in deference to our guests. Over the next several evenings, my prayers would touch on the foundational aspects of God and our relationship with Him.

The Love of God (BRIGHT STAR)

All loving and merciful God, we offer thanks for your abundant favor that you never cease to shed upon our lives. In ways too numerous to count we are the benefactors of your loving-kindness.

Your great love for us keeps us from the dangers woven into the fabric of our work. For as soon as we take them for granted, they appear, they pop up without warning seeking to frustrate our plans or bring about injury. Thank you for keeping them far from us today.

May we humble ourselves in your presence so we may see with our eyes and understand in our hearts all the benefits of your love.
In your Loving Name we pray,

Amen.

21 October

"REVEILLE, REVEILLE! ALL HANDS HEAVE OUT!
BREAKFAST FOR THE CREW!"

From: CHSYDNOR@HU
To: Undisclosed Recipients

Subject: FW: The Seventh Letter from the President (AME Chaplain's Association)

Dear Colleagues,

On behalf of all of the forward deployed chaplains involved in Operation Enduring Freedom, I would like to extend my sincere appreciation for the way you have kept us in your prayers, in touch with our church, and informed about current events back home. Your sustained effort has served to remind us that we are loved and supported by you as well as the American people.

We now live in a different world. Even though many of us may struggle to remember how our lives were before September 11, 2001, we no longer have the privilege to relish the relative innocence of that time. The heinous attacks on the World Trade Center and the Pentagon were the worst acts of violence perpetuated upon American soil and have shaken our country to its core. Perhaps the intention of the terrorists was to bring the collective will and conscience of our nation down to its knees. However, they never predicted what would happen once we got there. We began to pray: First, cries of grief and utter anguish over the despicable act itself and for the sense-less loss of life; then prayers of remembrance offered for all the victims and unexpected heroes, untold and unaccounted; petitions of healing and unity followed and eventually intercessions for strength for the nation and pro-tection for the members of the military who are and will be sent into harm's way. Throughout all these requests, our God has been completely faithful for he knows no other way to relate to those who call upon Him.

As I mentioned earlier, I am not the only chaplain who is forward deployed to the Middle East. Here is a list of others who are on the "Tip of the Spear":

LTCOL Ashford – USAF – Turkey
LCDR Taylor – USN – Spain
CAPT Pinkney – USAF – (undisclosed location)
LT Jennings Harrison – USN – USS KITTY HAWK (CV-63)
LT Valcourt – USN – USS VELLA GULF (CG-72)

I am aboard the USS SHREVEPORT (LPD-12). However, due to our current security posture, I as well as others, cannot disclose any future operational contingencies. From all accounts, though, we are all doing well as we provide critical spiritual support for the men and women of the armed forces.

In closing, I would like to personally thank those of you who have kept in touch with me since my departure in September. Your messages have never ceased to bring encouragement and inspiration. Also, pray for our families and loved ones back home. The special burden that they bear is perhaps more difficult than the one we incur at the execution of our duties.

May the Lord bless and keep you in His loving care!

Yours in Christ,

David R. Brown
Lieutenant, U.S. Navy
Chaplain Corps

President, AME Chaplain's Association

"Prayer Changes Things!"
Cal Sydnor, D. Min.
Assistant Professor of Ethics and Religion
The Leadership Institute
Hampton University

Egyptian soldiers carrying a Zodiac speedboat in the Well Deck

"SET CONDITION 1-ALPHA FOR WELL DECK OPERATIONS! SET CONDITION 1-ALPHA FOR WELL DECK OPERATIONS!"

Another long day of Well Deck Ops was ahead of us in support of BRIGHT STAR. The Egyptian soldiers took their CRRCs from the ship to the beach to conduct amphibious assault training. They were scheduled to return to the ship late in the day, overnight onboard, and do it all again in the morning.

I went down to the Well Deck from my stateroom to observe their departure. I passed a few soldiers on Mess Deck who called out to me, "*Dawoud! Dawoud*!" I acknowledged them with the greeting of "peace," in Arabic. Again, on the ladderwell on the way down to the Well Deck, I spoke "peace," to some more soldiers. It was more of the same once I entered the Well Deck, where several series of soldiers were amassed waiting for their CRRCs to take them to the shore.

God, please show me how to leverage this connection with the soldiers for you.

In Praise of our Sovereign God (BRIGHT STAR)

O Sovereign God, Creator of all life, whose speech brought into existence the heavens and the earth, whose will the wind, water, and sky obey, whose hands hold both time and eternity; we offer you the highest praise!

Your sovereignty allows us to plan and hope for the best while your grace allows us to respond and rebound when things do not work in our favor. As the day unfolded, you revealed to us our designed path; we amended our schedule to comply and conform.

May we continue to utilize our experience and preparedness as we seek to accept your will in any and every situation.

In your Sovereign Name we pray,

Amen.

"TAPS, TAPS, LIGHTS OUT! ALL HANDS TURN TO YOUR BUNKS. MAINTAIN SILENCE ABOUT THE DECKS. TAPS!"

22 October
"SET CONDITION 1-ALPHA FOR WELL DECK OPERATIONS! SET CONDITION 1-ALPHA FOR WELL DECK OPERATIONS!"

From: K@HOME
To: CHAPS@SHREVEPORT

Subject: Hello!

Hey Chaplain!

I heard you have some visitors onboard these days. Wow! What an opportunity! Have you been able to share the gospel with any of them? I will pray that you get many chances to do so. I just recently read a book called *A Christian's Response to Islam*, written by a missionary to Iran who spent forty-something years there! Some of the things he mentioned were that Muslims have no assurance of salvation; they do not know if God is pleased with their life until after they die and face judgment. That is a life of uncertainty and desperation, I am sure. He also talked about a conversation he had in which he asked a man if he thought love was an important quality. "Of course," the man responded. So the author asked him to compare the Koran's statements on love with the Bible's. The author cited the book of 1 John, which speaks of love in almost every aspect in just a few verses. On the other hand, the man could only find a few references about love in the Koran. We have a God who loves us and promises salvation! What good news that is!

I hope you are encouraged these days. I am praying that the forces of darkness on SHREVEPORT are held at bay and defeated. Keep on in the fight, Brother!

Love in Christ,
Kay

This was a challenging message from a former ship's officer, now on shore duty in Norfolk. Kay was a dear sister in the Lord who had detached from the ship earlier in the year. Whenever she was not on Watch and could attend worship services, she did. Her message made me face my dual responsibility—to my faith and my profession. As a Christian, this was a golden opportunity to witness to so many that did not know Christ as Lord and Savior. As a chaplain, witnessing, known as proselytizing, was completely unethical, particularly, in a religiously plural environment like the Navy. On top of this, I was under no obligation to provide Religious Ministry for the Egyptians because they were not American forces. I had no trouble holding all these competing interests in balance. My challenge was to live the gospel—not just with the Egyptians but also with the crew—and daily surrender my life to the control of the Holy Spirit so that others might see Jesus in my actions and attitude.

News of a Port Visit

It was official: We were heading to Italy for our next liberty port. Sometime around the end of the month, we would come into port at La Maddalena, Sardinia. It would be a short visit, just over forty-eight hours, but a welcome break after all our hard work during BRIGHT STAR. In my deckplate visitations, I shared the news with many sailors. They were glad to hear about this since the word had not trickled down to their workspaces yet. In sharing, I realized that God was showing me more of the world, just as he had promised at the beginning of my career. First, going cross-country, then Japan, the Caribbean, the breadth of the Atlantic, Africa and Europe—and more to follow!

"DAILY PRAYER MEETING WILL BE HELD IN SACC AT 1230."

I ventured outside the ship to get some fresh air. I made my way past the Flight Deck, Boat Deck and all the way up to the level of the Signal Bridge at the top of the ship. At once, the sunny skies and warm sea breezes were clearing my head. In the distance, I could see the shoreline and thought how good it would have been to set foot on African soil. I could also see some of the CRRCs heading back to the ship.

Tonight would be the Egyptians' last night onboard ship. In spite of the picture our anxieties had painted, everything went very well. The soldiers were simply courteous and professional. Besides, the multiple years in which the Egyptians had hosted BRIGHT STAR probably made them more used to training with American forces than vice versa.

From: CHAPS@SHREVEPORT
To: K@HOME

Re: Hello!

Kay,

Thanks for reaching out! Your advice from the book you mentioned offers some great conversation points. Thus far, I am on very good terms with a group of about eight officers. They call me *Dawoud*, which is pronounced Da-ood. Please pray for me on this last evening together.

The ministry aboard ship is truly expanding. There was one point last week where God put it in the spotlight for all to see. Before our guests came aboard, there was some anxiety over offending their Islamic cultural habits. One area of concern for the CO was the Evening Prayer at Sea. One evening at OPS/INTEL, he publicly mentioned he thought we should postpone the prayer until the guests departed. After he said this, I went back to my stateroom to pray, asking God to give me the words to convince the CO it was a bad idea to cancel the prayer. Praise God the prayers have continued and I learned that our guests have been listening too.

Our work out here is coming to a close. Soon we will be headed for another adventure. Please keep us in your prayers.

Love in Christ,
Chaps

About 1845

After dinner, I went outside the skin of the ship to get some fresh air and catch the fading sunlight. As I exited the Hangar Bay onto the Flight Deck, I heard a commotion, sounds of singing and clapping one deck above me. I saw a crowd of about thirty sailors and soldiers celebrating something on the port side weather deck. I climbed the ladderwell leading to the location and found an impromptu celebration led by the Egyptian soldiers. They had formed a circle, the soldiers singing in unison—in Arabic—and clapping in syncopation with one in the middle of the circle doing some sort of traditional dancing. The soldier in the middle danced for a few more minutes then changed positions with another from the circle, who continued to dance to the music. The sailors were getting a kick out of this. Some were even clapping, assisting with keeping the beat. I found one of the Egyptian officers on the outskirts and I asked him, "What is the celebration about?"

"We are celebrating the end of the exercise and our last night on ship," he said.

"Where did the soldiers learn to dance like that?" I asked.

"Oh! It is dance we learned as children," he said.

"Well, it looks like a lot of fun," I said.

The celebration continued with another soldier dancing in the middle exchange. The Egyptian officer leaned over and asked, "Are you going home after we are done?"

"No, we are continuing with our deployment. We won't get home until sometime next year," I said.

"So you will miss Christmas?" he asked.

"Yes. What do you know about Christmas?" I asked.

"Oh! We celebrate Christmas in Egypt," he said. "All the merchants will decorate their shops with lights and many people will exchange gifts."

"We do the same in America but Christians see Christmas as the time to celebrate Jesus' birth," I said.

"Yes, we know Jesus. He is a prophet and a great teacher," he said.

"Yes, I agree, however, for Christians, he is more. He is our Lord and Savior, the Son of God," I said.

At this he smiled but had no response, turning his attention back to the celebration. This conversation between us was as unexpected to me as the celebration. I reflected later in the evening that this was a moment of witnessing brought by the Lord. It did not seem unethical or offensive.

"OPS/INTEL BRIEF, WARDROOM"

Tonight's brief covered ENDEX—End of Exercise—where the Egyptian soldiers along with all amphibious, ground, and air forces would storm the beach in one grand, coordinated assault. It was a tight fit. All of our officers as well as the leading officers from the Egyptian forces were present. At the end of the brief, the captain arose and asked the commanding officer from the Egyptian forces to join him at the front of the room. He made some commending remarks about how professional his soldiers were and how well they performed during the exercise and he presented him with an engraved plaque from our ship, which garnered obligatory applause from everyone assembled. The captain then invited all the officers to come up and bid farewell to the commanding officer and his staff. We queued up, from senior to junior officers, to shake hands with them. When it was my turn to greet the commanding officer, he shook my hand but pulled me close until we were chest-to-chest. He looked me in the eye and said, "Da-oooood!" I reached around his shoulder with my free arm and gave him a man hug saying, "God bless you, my brother. God bless you!" His one-word greeting, compounded in sentiment, lingered with me even as I moved on to greet the rest of his staff.

"TATTOO, TATTOO! LIGHTS OUT IN FIVE MINUTES! STAND BY FOR THE EVENING PRAYER."

God our provider (BRIGHT STAR)

O God, you are our Great Provider!

What is in our lives that you have not given to us? Is the sun's warmth controlled by thermostat? Have the seas stayed calm on their own? Wasn't the rest we received much needed? And what shall we say of our food, clothing, shelter, or any other things we take for granted? Have you not displayed your providence in all your ways?

The answers are "Yes" and "Amen." For we know of no one as faithful as you. You are like a loving parent that always knows and does what is best for his children.

Thank you for meeting all our needs with a bounty of blessings that never runs out.

In your Mighty Name we pray,

Amen.

23 October

"SET CONDITION 1-ALPHA FOR WELL DECK OPERATIONS! SET CONDITION 1-ALPHA FOR WELL DECK OPERATIONS!"

0925
From: CHAPS@SHREVEPORT
To: RB@HOME

Hey!

The Egyptians are departing today. I am going down to the Well Deck to bid them farewell. It was a great experience to have them aboard and they opened the eyes of a lot of crewmembers.

The pictures I sent last night are of me with the Egyptian Officers in the Wardroom. The short one standing next to me in the lounge was the commander of the 743rd Tank Battalion. He and I really clicked. It was funny: he even knew the "soul brother" handshake. Even though his English wasn't great, I watched as he gave the normal handshake to the captain and others but he gave me the real deal, "What's Happening, Brotha?" greeting. He did not have to explain either. I knew exactly what he was saying. It is amazing what translates between cultures!

We have a long day of back-loading the Marines ahead of us. The final demonstration ashore is a pretty big deal. I heard the Commandant of the Marine Corps will be there to observe along with all the big brass from the Egyptian Army.

I will keep lifting you and our son up in prayer. Take care and talk to you soon.

Love,
Chaps

Well Deck Departure

Some of the officers gathered in the Well Deck to see the Egyptians off the ship. First Lieutenant Adams and Doc Buxton were among the few that shook hands and posed for pictures with the soldiers. The exchanges between us were jovial, even somewhat poignant. The soldiers donned their float coats and helmets and boarded their CRRCs—eight to a boat—and departed the ship.

The Back-Load Begins (BRIGHT STAR ends)

Gracious Lord, bless us tonight as the back load of personnel and equipment continues. Our guests have debarked, BRIGHT STAR has come to an end, and we await the safe arrival of all our teammates. Their presence back aboard allows the ship to resemble its true nature and character.

Help us to realize a few things about this evolution:
The work is arduous; it will take strength, patience,
and flexibility through the night and into the next day.
The work is hazardous; we pray our experience will give us an edge against the risks surrounding us. The work is necessary;
we desire to finish like we started; together and intact.

Lord, we require nothing short of your hand to provide for our needs.
Fortify us, protect us, and reunite us in safety.

This we pray in your Holy Name,

Amen.

Egyptian Commanders salute and wave "Goodbye"

24 October

Hey!

Hope you had a great day yesterday!

We are anchored off the coast back-loading all the Marines and their equipment. This evolution will take all day to complete. Once we are done we will pull up the anchor and head back to sea. We will spend the next several days sailing to Italy to get our feet on dry ground. It has been about twenty-five days at sea and the crew is ready for a port visit.

There is nothing more from the chaplain corps detailer as far as orders are concerned. I am going to send him a friendly reminder asking what specific type of duty is at the Naval Station in Norfolk. I am sure it is the chapel but I would like to have him confirm this.

I received a letter in the mail from the mother of Fireman White, the Sailor who was killed in South Carolina. I wrote to her back in September just to stay in touch and to let her know we had not forgotten about her son. She mentioned she is at a point where she is able to thank the Lord for the twenty-one years He had given her son. She also mentioned that all who were directly/indirectly involved have been arrested. She concluded with a standing invitation: We have a place to eat and stay if we are ever in South Carolina.

Stay encouraged!
Chaps

Satisfaction and Continuance

Gracious Lord, your blessing of favor has been upon us throughout this entire journey even through the conclusion of BRIGHT STAR. We have satisfied all operational requirements in relative safety and are prepared to continue our journey.

We learned some valuable lessons, had some unforgettable experiences, and have grown in ways too early to measure. Growth has not been confined to the eastern Mediterranean, though. Those on the homefront have become a little wiser, a little stronger, and a bit more resourceful. Perhaps some have even experienced renewal in their faith.

Whichever way we look at it, you have allowed us to come to a point of continuance—moments to take stock and share sea stories, but ultimately to cast our gaze upon the horizon. For therein lies what you are about to bring into our future.

Thank you, Lord, for everything you allowed us to accomplish and for the opportunity to move forward.

This we pray in your Holy Name,

Amen.

-11-

LA MADDALENA
Last chance at Liberty

October 25, 2001

La Maddalena, Italy offered a welcomed break right after BRIGHT STAR. We all sensed it was going to our last liberty port for a while. Sailors and Marines were definitely going to make the most of their free time ashore. My mind was on two things, cuisine and Christmas shopping for souvenirs. This was the chance to have authentic Italian food and to ensure that my immediate family members would have a piece of Italy under their Christmas tree this year.

Uniting Through Reading Program

Before departing Norfolk, RP1 Bates and I received a brief on a program called Uniting Through Reading (UTR). We learned that the whole mission sought to ease the burden of the physical and psychological separation of deployment for military families through the experience of reading aloud together. Here is how it worked: Sailors and Marines would volunteer to have themselves privately videotaped reading aloud a children's book. They would mail the videotape and book home to their family, who would play the tape and have the child or children follow along. It was easy to see how this program strengthened family ties and encouraged literacy and a love for reading.

We were ready to start UTR onboard the ship but I had to give the XO a final brief.

From: CHAPS@SHREVEPORT
To: XO@SHREVEPORT

Subject: Uniting Through Reading update

Sir,

The Supply Officer reminded me that he intends to purchase the videotapes for the Unite Through Reading Program when we come into port at La Maddalena. Once that is done, there is nothing preventing us from commencing the program.

Here are several issues that should be considered before we begin:

ORIENTATION: I have a fifteen-minute CD presentation I would like for you to review and some basic background information about the program that you may look over at your leisure. I will place it in your inbox today. This folder can be forwarded to the CO.

LOGISTICAL SUPPORT: We have already fired a warning shot to the petty officer in charge of Site TV that this program will be coming his way. He informed us that he is ready to support. However, he mentioned that his taping machine handles VHS-C tapes, which are an entirely different format and size than VHS tapes. If we have a VCR that handles VHS tapes he can proceed without a problem. I immediately thought about requesting the VCR in the Wardroom only because of its lack of use among the members. I think it has been there since 19 September without anyone even touching it, not even the Marines. Also, that VCR has two input and output jacks in the front that should work perfectly.

TIME SCHEDULE: Obviously, we would create a schedule that supports operational demands. They suggest that each video takes about fifteen minutes per person. On WHIDBEY ISLAND, they utilize a signup sheet and each member goes to the Site TV studio to do their taping at the appointed time.

ADVERTISEMENT: Once you have seen the CD, you will see why it will be an effective way to advertise this program to the crew. A 1MC announcement and POD notes should be compulsory and a fireside plug from the captain wouldn't hurt.

EXECUTION: The goal is to keep this as low maintenance and user friendly as possible. As you read through the material you will notice articles heralding the success of the program from various shipboard commands. You will also notice there seems to be a larger organizational structure behind it. It is not my intention to recreate such a model aboard SHREVEPORT. This is something RP1 and I can coordinate. There is an excellent example of how I would like things to go displayed on the "Full Circle" diagram located in the folder.

MATERIALS: We have the space and taping equipment. We are awaiting the purchase of the tapes, though. The only sticking point is that I have about twenty children's books—surely not enough to go around. If the response is big, and I believe it will be, we could have members just read, send the tape home, and request that the return package include another book. Then the member could read and send both the video and book home.

END STATE: If we can get locked on now, tapes could be made and sent home in time for Thanksgiving. Then return tapes from home could reach the ship by Christmas, which would be a huge morale boost for both ends.

Very respectfully,
Chaplain Brown

From: ITCS@SHREVEPORT
To: CHAPS@SHREVEPORT

Subject: FW: OUR SHIPMATE/SAILOR/FRIEND/BROTHER IN HIS FINAL RESTING PLACE

Sir,

I received the below report from one of our former officers. It is about the funeral for our fallen shipmate, IT2 Bishundat. Please take moment and read it over. Thanks!

V/r,
ITCS Chestnut

Senior Chief Chestnut,

I am honored that I had the opportunity to attend 1T2(SW) Bishundat's Memorial Service. It was truly a sight to see. I have never in my entire life attended a funeral service as large as the one for our fallen shipmate. There were people from all walks of life. Bishundat touched so many lives in his short time on this place we call earth. I want to try to recap some of the events for you:

- On October 5th, The Naval Computer and Telecommunications Station at the Pentagon in Washington DC held a Memorial Service for all our fallen shipmates including Bishundat. The president posthumously awarded him the Purple Heart and the Navy Commendation Medal.

- On October 8th, there was an Indian Celebration with his family. After that celebration everyone went to the funeral home for the last viewing which was closed casket. The funeral home then took his body around town and for a final drive through his old neighborhood and by his house. They returned and headed to Arlington National Cemetery. The line of cars was approximately six to eight miles long with police escort all the way through Maryland to Virginia, and then was picked up by the Park Police in Washington, DC. It took about 300 police officers from five counties to get us all to Bishundat's final resting

place. As you can tell by the size of the funeral, it took a lot of coordination with local and even federal authorities. Just the way Bishundat would have like it—super-sized!

- On October 17th, his family held a service in his honor in his hometown of Waldorf, Maryland. It was a beautiful event. There was an ambassador from his native country in South America, the county sheriff, football and basketball coaches, pastors, schoolteachers, doctors, lawyers, sailors, officers, schoolmates, his entire family including those from his native land, and the entire neighborhood. I really believe almost the entire town must have attended. During the service numerous people had words to share about Bish including myself. He knew everyone in his town and left a huge footprint on all of them. After the service, everyone went to his parents' home for some great food. What a feast!

Upon arriving at the front gate of Arlington National Cemetery, the cars from the procession entered. The Navy took over from there. What a superb ceremony! Full honors: words from the captain, words from the admiral, words from the family pastor, reading the citation for the Navy Commendation Medal and for the Purple Heart, the bugler played, the color guard, and the gun salute. I have to tell you this was truly an event that will stick with me for the rest of my life. After all was said and done, the casket remained on the top of the grass and family and friends did not want to leave. It was like they did not want to let him be committed to the ground. I remember during the service, I looked around and out of the hundreds of people there, all were sad and most had tears running down their faces. I paused for a few minutes, took a deep breath, and looked across the cemetery in the direction of the Pentagon. I remember getting angry because our shipmate was killed there. I immediately pulled myself together and thought of you and the SHREVEPORT. Then for some reason, everything was all right because I know you all were on the tip of the spear and would serve our great country with the utmost of your ability while you are deployed. On my drive home, I could only think of our shipmate and how he impacted my life. Bish was a great person, Sailor, brother, and friend. I miss him!!!

A friend of the family made a beautiful video for the Bishundat Family. It contains great pictures and songs chosen by the family. I have a copy and will send it to the ship so you can share it with all the sailors. I also have a few buttons with Bish on them that we all wore during this trying time. The family gave me newspapers to send to the ship as well. Senior, I have to tell you to be prepared because the entire family is coming to visit the new Bishundat Computer Room upon your return to Norfolk. Please be ready to receive them. They talked of you the entire time I was there. We must go see them once you return home. We are a part of this family. They love you for what you have done and for what you meant to their son. I shared plenty of conversations with them about you. Take care!

From: CHAPS@SHREVEPORT
To: ITCS@SHREVEPORT

Re: FW:

Senior,

WOW! What an awesome account. Moving, just moving! Thanks for sharing it with me.

Respectfully,
Chaps

From: ITCS@SHREVEPORT
To: CHAPS@SHREVEPORT

Re: FW:

Chaps,

The people that we come across like IT2 Bishundat and his family are what make my naval career just awesome! He is one Sailor whom I will always have a definite sense of pride. He will never be forgotten. I know I have always given the personnel in my department and division 100 percent. These kids are my kids and their parents expect me to take care of them. I promise them that I will. When I see a young kid come aboard ship, a little scared and immature and watch him grow into a very respectful young man, it is just awesome from my perspective.

V/r,
ITCS Chestnut

I read the account a few more times just to let it sink in. Bish was a special kid. Gone but not forgotten.

Late Evening
From: CHAPS@SHREVEPORT
To: RB@HOME

Subject: Satellite and approaching storm

Hey!

Sorry for the cut offs last night. The captain announced we are heading into a storm and the next couple of days will be rough out here. The satellite connection does not work as well when we are moving around and when there is bad weather. If you noticed, the last couple of times I sent messages from Egypt the connection was clear and uninterrupted. Every day was sunshine in the mid 80's off the coast.

I pray often for your strength. I praise God for the Herculean job you have done raising our son. My days have been filled with deployment stuff but I would much prefer to be there to handle the load with you.

Trust in the Lord with all your heart. And not lean on your own understanding; in all your ways acknowledge Him and he will make your paths straight. (Proverbs 3:5)

Everything is going to be all right. God has been completely faithful and will continue to be towards us. Draw strength from His strength.

I will try to email again when things are more stable.

Love,
Chaps

27 November

"REVEILLE, REVEILLE! ALL HANDS HEAVE OUT!
BREAKFAST FOR THE CREW!"

From: CHAPS@SHREVEPORT
To: RB@HOME

Good Morning!

We are well on our way to La Maddalena! If you are familiar with Italy's geography, you will notice the bottom of the country is shaped like a boot. If you follow the tip of the boot slightly northwest you will notice two islands there. The smaller one on top is Corsica, which belongs to France. The larger one is Sardinia. There is a small Navy base there called La Maddalena and we will be stopping there on Monday for a few days. We are looking forward to the break after nearly a month at sea.

The heavy seas are starting to kick in but I am doing fine. My sea legs are strong, thank the Lord, so I will be alright.

Love,
Chaps

About 2000

I received my first request for religious accommodation this evening from a Sailor who was a practitioner of the Wicca Faith. He specifically requested to conduct a ritual called "Samhain," an ancient festival marking the end of the harvest season. Wicca is a modern pagan religion and is typically duo-theistic, worshipping both a god and goddess. Wicca is also an officially recognized religion by the Department of Defense (DoD). So from a DoD perspective, Wicca was not any different from Christianity, Buddhism, Islam, or Judaism.

Along with his request, he offered a sample message about the ritual he wanted to have posted in the Plan-of-the-Day. He proposed it should take place on the evening of 30 October 2001. It was important for me to advise the CO/XO concerning this request.

From: CHAPS@SHREVEPORT
To: XO@SHREVEPORT

Subject: Religious Accommodation Request

Sir,

I received a request from a Sailor who is a member of the Wiccan Faith and he would like to conduct a ritual on October 30 aboard ship. I asked him to put together an explanation and order of service, then come in and verbally explain in detail exactly what would take place.

Although he is not a command sponsored lay reader, he did mention that he served as one on his previous ship. On the day he checked in with me, which was about three months ago, I informed him that in order to become a lay reader he would have to have an endorsement from his religious body, go through lay reader training with me, and obtain written approval from the CO. Lt. j.g. Depke, who is Roman Catholic, and Chief Ducass, who is Protestant, had to adhere to the same standard.

In short, it is a situation I would like to discuss further before we announce via POD.

Very respectfully,
Chaplain Brown

From: XO@SHREVEPORT
To: CHAPS@SHREVEPORT

Re: Religious Accommodation Request

Chaplain,

I realize that October 30th is an important day for the Wiccans. If there is a ritual being conducted on EMORY S. LAND, I would be more than glad to authorize Wiccans from SHREVEPORT to attend. In my mind, this would be preferable to conducting the event here.

If we decide to authorize, the CO and I will need to be engaged in the content of the services.

R,
XO

To be certain, the Wiccan population aboard the ship was pretty low. They were in the minority and I, being African-American, understood that position. Funny thing, though, there is nothing minor about the God I serve or his ability to save and bless His people. Thus, there is nothing minor about my faith. It is close to my heart. It is my very life. I suspected that, at the very least, this Sailor felt the same way about his faith as well as other sailors from his faith group.

Lord, help me to handle this situation well, to do what is in order and decency, and not bring reproach to your Name. Amen.

Wisdom

Gracious Lord, we need your wisdom to give us guidance in this life.

For all the decisions that are out of our hands but are in our lap,
Lord, grant us wisdom.

For situations that require immediate attention but not a hasty response,
Lord, grant us wisdom.

To uphold the truth even when deceit is more convenient,
Lord, grant us wisdom.

For actions prompted by obligation to duty rather than devotion to self,
Lord, grant us wisdom.

For the ability to speak words that bring healing instead of harm,
Lord, grant us wisdom.

To acknowledge what is right, to desire what is right, and the will to
do the same,
Lord, grant us wisdom.

For all the tough calls, suspended verdicts, or fence straddling, when we no
longer know where to turn or how to make the next move, when peace of
mind eludes us because we are torn between two or more opinions, please,
Lord, grant us wisdom.

Amen.

28 October
From: XO@SHREVEPORT
To: CO@SHREVEPORT
Cc: CHAPS@SHREVEPORT

Subject: Wiccan Ritual

Captain,

I directed Chaplain Brown to check with LAND's chaplain, and see if the Wiccans are holding a Samhain ritual on their ship. If so, our best option is sending our sailors over there for the ritual. If not, Chaplain Brown will discuss with you the advisability of accommodating this ritual. Obviously, if we did hold it, we would need specific details on conduct of the ritual.

Although this Sailor has provided the chaplain with a more detailed ritual plan, the fact remains that he is not a command-sponsored lay reader.

V/R
XO

The captain could not have been more explicit in his decision.

From: CO@SHREVEPORT
To: XO@SHREVEPORT
Cc: CHAPS@SHREVEPORT

Re: Wiccan Ritual

No command-sponsored Wiccan rituals anytime/anyplace. Non-negotiable.

From: CHAPS@SHREVEPORT
To: CO@SHREVEPORT
Cc: XO@SHREVEPORT

Re: Wiccan Ritual

Aye, Aye, Sir!

Just a reminder, Wicca is a DoD-listed religion. Otherwise, I would have never brought this concern to your attention.

With all due respect, I am obligated to inform this Sailor that he is within his rights to seek advice from our Equal Opportunity Officer as well as legal counsel from the Staff-Judge Advocate at Amphibious Group Two back in Norfolk.

Very respectfully,
Chaplain Brown

The captain really meant "Non-negotiable" because he offered no response to my last email.

Late Afternoon
From: JAB@HOME
To: CHAPS@SHREVEPORT

Subject: "Jumping the Broom!"

Hey Bro, just wanted to say hello and let you know that I got engaged! I popped the question yesterday, Saturday the 27th, and she said yes! We stopped by the house, told Mom, and sat for about an hour afterwards. She was very excited and happy for us both.

Then we drove up here to Pennsylvania to be with her parents. I asked Mom to come up and celebrate with us, but she was not up to the trip. I know she really did want to be here though. I think she really needed to rest up some anyway.

We are going to be making plans for the wedding ASAP. You are still going to be my best man and will be making arrangements according with our last talk about it. I know you may not be able to disclose your ship's movements or return date at this time. Please let me know, when it is safe and feasible for you to do so, if the dates we previously discussed have changed.

I hope and pray you are well and are in good spirits. I got that piece of snail mail off to you finally. I sent it last Tuesday, the 23rd. So keep an eye out for it. I need to know if you can receive attachments to your email on the ship.

I would like to send you a photo of her and the ring. I want to send it in an email if you have the ability to view photos too. Well I have to run for now. I am off to church with Jean and her family soon. You take care, be well, God Bless, and I will get back to you soon.

Love,
JAB

From: CHAPS@SHREVEPORT
To: JAB@HOME

Re: Jumping the Broom!

Congratulations Bro!

I am very happy for you! May the Lord's richest blessings be upon you as you plan and prepare for life as a married couple!

Please continue to pray for our safety. Thanks again for letting me in on the great news!

Love,
Chaps

From: CHAPS@SHREVEPORT
To: RB@HOME

Hey!

I got an email from my brother confirming he is engaged to be married. I am happy for the both of them. He did not mention a date but I suspect it will be sometime after I get back home.

We had another great day at worship. About twenty showed up for service. The ship decided to hold Halloween early because we will be in port on the actual day. There was a Steel Beach Picnic, basketball games, weightlifting competition, and costume contest. Derby won in his weight class during the weightlifting competition.

I am wondering what kind of souvenirs I should pick up in La Maddalena.

Any suggestions? I should be able to call you on a regular phone. They say the base is very small and that the attraction is taking the ferry across the bay into town. We are scheduled to get in at mid-morning.

Love,
Chaps

From: RB@HOME
To: CHAPS@SHREVEPORT

As for gifts, I don't know. I think any souvenir from another country would be appropriate and would be greatly appreciated. Speaking of gifts, what are we doing about Christmas gifts this year? Think about it. If you do not have the time or ability to shop over there as we planned, then gift certificates are always a winner. Let me know and we can discuss.

Thanks for your continued thoughts and prayers.

Love ya!
RB

From: CHAPS@SHREVEPORT
To: CHAPS@ESL

Subject: Question about Wiccan Services

Sir,

I am Chaplain David Brown from the USS SHREVEPORT (LPD-12). I have a question concerning Wiccan Services aboard the EMORY S. LAND (ESL). Tuesday evening, October 30th, is the Wiccan celebration of Samhain. Will the ESL be conducting any ritual observance at that time? If so, please reply at your earliest convenience about the time and specific location of the event. Our command would prefer to allow our crewmembers to come to the ESL to attend.

Very respectfully,
Chaplain Brown

From: CHAPS@ESL
To: CHAPS@SHREVEPORT

Subject: Re: Question about Wiccan Services

Chaplain Brown,

The ESL does not have a formal, practicing Wiccan community. A few folks have broached the subject of Wiccan worship in the past but there has been no follow through on their part. So, in answer to your request there will be no Wiccan observance of Samhain on the ESL.

I look forward to meeting you upon your arrival in La Maddalena. Our offices are located on the 2-53-2-L near the vending machine area outboard. My deputy chaplain and I are delighted to be your hosts while you are tended to our good ship.

God Bless You!
V/r,

Command Chaplain
USS EMORY S. LAND (AS-39)

From: CHAPS@SHREVEPORT
To: CHAPS@ESL

Re: Question about Wiccan Services

Sir,

Thanks for your prompt reply! We have the same situation except ours is headed in the other direction; the community desires to gather. We have one Sailor who checked aboard three months ago and immediately identified himself as Wiccan. Further, he explained to me that he was a lay reader aboard another vessel. I explained to him that if he wanted to do the same here he would need current endorsement from his faith group, undergo lay reader training with me, and receive the CO's written endorsement permitting him to conduct lay services. He has not completed any of the above requirements. However, he made a request on Friday to celebrate Samhain aboard our ship. The captain effectively denied his request.

I have informed the captain of the instruction pertaining to lay readers and Wicca's status as a DoD-listed religion within the Armed Forces.

Thanks again for your advice concerning this matter. I am looking forward to meeting you as well.

Very respectfully,
Chaplain Brown

That was the end of the matter. After it was over, I thought about how many Christians back home would have cringed at the fact that I had gone such lengths for a practitioner of a faith group so antithetical to our own. However, it was my professional obligation as a Navy Chaplain to do so, to protect the free exercise of religion, and to advise the captain on matters that impact his Command Religious Program. It was my duty to treat him and his request with the utmost respect and dignity. I made peace with this, on a personal level, by taking the spiritual high ground.

What if my life was the only Bible this Sailor would ever read, the only gospel he would ever experience, or the only Jesus he would ever see?

In situations like this, I also had a spiritual responsibility to have my conduct sow the seed and let God decide upon which type of ground it would fall. (Luke 8:5-15)

Pulling into La Maddalena (Thankfulness)

Gracious Lord, as we prepare for this port visit into La Maddalena, we are thankful for the good fortune we have experienced over the past several weeks. We have worked hard to come to this point and are aware that coming into port is a special privilege.

It has been close to a month since we were in a position poised to enjoy liberty. What a wonderful opportunity we have tonight to pause and reflect, for all your goodness towards us!

So as we embrace the prospect of liberty, bless us with safety throughout the port visit and always keep us within your care.

Amen.

29 October
From: CHAPS@SHREVEPORT
To: RB@HOME

Subject: Arrival at La Maddalena!

We are here! La Maddalena is one of four small islands off the coast of Sardinia. It's rocky, rugged, and hilly landscape reminds me of the high desert. Really! The island looks like the terrain on Amboy Road right after you pass the I-40 underpass and into the Mojave Preserve. I will send some pictures tomorrow and you will see immediately what I am talking about.

You have to take a ferry from the ship to get over to the town because it is across the bay from the Naval Base. The base itself is not much to speak about. It is actually spread out over the island. The REC center, Navy Federal, and the gym are by the pier. The housing area and chapel are located in another area and the exchange in another. I hope to see it all but without a car the distances are too great.

A group of us had dinner in the downtown area and I observed that eating is an event for the Italian people. When we sat down to dine, we could not bring a fast food, "Waiter, where is the check?" mentality to the table. We had to be prepared to stay a while and savor a five-course meal, with fifteen to twenty minutes at the completion of each course to engage in laughter and conversation. Wine, good wine I am told, is compulsory and there were several bottles on the table, more than enough for everyone seated, yet, no one was drunk. I had some of the best Prosciutto—tender, smoky, and salty—I have ever tasted in my life!

We ended up walking around the town for the rest of the evening. The businesses and homes surrounding the waterfront are done in the Spanish colonial style just like Kelso Depot and old cobblestone streets, which are very narrow, run in between them. It feels and looks like Old San Juan, Puerto Rico.

I am still on the souvenir Christmas present search. I have found a few prospects and will continue to search. The Lire, the Italian currency, is worth about half as much as a dollar. The current rate is 2,100 Lire to the dollar. That means more buying power for my money.

I hope your day has gone well. I will try to give you a call once we go on liberty. Be patient, though. Sailors and Marines mob the phones on base.

I love you very much!
Chaps

31 October
From: CHAPS@SHREVEPORT
To: RB@HOME

Subject: A couple of things...

Hey!

I received your package today! It is the one with the pictures, postcard, news-paper clippings, and refrigerator magnets. What a nice surprise. I am saving the news articles for when we get underway so I will have some interesting reading to look forward too.

Everything is going well in Italy. Today is picture day out in town. I am going out with First Lieutenant Adams to get some digital photos. I will send them to you later in the day.

The vendors from the NEX came aboard ship with some terrific Italian souvenirs. The quality is outstanding so I think I am going to do some Christmas shopping. Not too much, just some good items primarily for our son, Mom, Mom and Dad and for yours truly.

Love,
Chaps

From: RB@HOME
To: CHAPS@SHREVEPORT

Re: A couple of things...

Now, I really wish I was there! Authentic Italian food, great shopping: Oh well, maybe on another leisure trip.

I am glad my small package came. I wish the other one with the goodies had arrived. Do not worry. I got another goody package off to you yesterday. Hopefully that one will arrive to you within the week.

Take care and I will hopefully talk to you soon. Happy shopping!

Love Ya,
RB

Early Evening
From: CHAPS@SHREVEPORT
To: RB@HOME

Re: A couple of things...

I have completed about 90 percent of our Christmas shopping today. I bought gifts for the following:

My Mom
Your Mom
My brothers and their wives

That leaves your brother, Dad, and the nephews and nieces. We can put our heads together about them and get gift certificates for the nephews and nieces.

We pull out tomorrow. It has been a great port visit and break for the crew. I am going to get some parting shots of the islands on our way out of the area.

Have a good night and I will talk to you soon.

Love,
Chaps

I did not let on to my wife how disturbed I was about how the evening really ended. At the ferry dock, there was a group of sailors holding up one of their shipmates. He was passed-drunk, barely coherent, seeming to drift in and out of consciousness. They eventually sat him down on the edge of the pier and began cleaning off the profuse vomit covering his shirt and pants. One of the sailors attending to him broke away and approached me with an indirect request for counseling on behalf of his inebriated shipmate. "Nope! I do not counsel drunken sailors," I responded. "Let him sober up and he can come see me in the morning." I also had a run-in with another drunken Sailor, a direct confrontation so upsetting that I could not go to sleep. I knew I had to contact his Department Head (DH) about the incident first thing in the morning.

01 November 2001
From: CHAPS@SHREVEPORT
To: DH@SHREVEPORT

Subject: Liberty Incident

DH,

I had a slight incident with one of your sailors last night while I was on liberty. After Chief Ducass, Senior Chief Anderson, and I finished dinner, we were on our way back to the ship when this Sailor and his Liberty Buddy greeted us. He had a comment for me and I told him I would try to address it. He said I was waking up his shipmates because my evening prayers were too loud. I thought this was a strange comment so I asked him what he meant. He said something to the effect, "Your prayers are too loud in the berthing spaces." I thought for a moment but what he said was not making sense. I realized that he may have had something to drink and my suspicions were correct. I told him that I would like to talk to him tomorrow aboard ship but that was not good enough for him at the time. I finally said, "Shipmate, a drunk man is a sober man talking! I will talk to you tomorrow aboard ship when you are sober." Then I abruptly left the scene.

We stopped in a store a few blocks away to buy post cards, when I came out this Sailor and his buddy were standing outside. He insisted on continuing the conversation. He even badgered me a bit by asking, "Is that it? Do I intimidate you? Is that it?" I gave him the same answer as I did earlier and left that scene as well.

Here is what I think about the whole thing: There may be a legitimate concern that he has about the volume of my evening prayers in the berthing areas. However, last night on liberty, with one of us under the influence, was not the time or place to discuss his concern. I will offer him the opportunity today to listen to where he is coming from and that I would be "all ears". I just wanted to give you some notice as his Department Head.

Respectfully,
Chaps

Aside from the influence of alcohol, I sensed there was an underlying spiritual matter to this situation. God was using my prayers to reach the crew and in doing so, it had unintended consequences. It seems that not everyone aboard ship was a fan of my evening prayers. It was no matter, though. I was not about to change the way I conducted the prayer. I stay close to the Lord to receive the prayer and I keep my mouth close to the microphone when I deliver it. For the latter point, I have heard the evening prayer delivered with the microphone at a normal distance about six to eight inches from the face and I could hardly hear it. This also means sailors and Marines about the ship can "heart-ly" hear it. My prayers ran deep, glory to God, which was a good thing.

Mid-Morning
From: SHIPMATE@SHREVEPORT
To: CHAPS@SHREVEPORT

Subject: (No subject)

Chaps,

I just came by your office and you were out and about. Also, I had a word with my Department Head and read the email he received from you regarding last night. My sincere apologies to you; my behavior was unacceptable toward a commissioned officer, a chaplain, and someone I admire. It was out of line and I hope you accept my apology.

From: CHAPS@SHREVEPORT
To: SHIPMATE@SHREVEPORT

Re:

Shipmate,

Apology accepted. As for the prayer matter, I am at your service and I am always available to listen to your perspective. You name the time and place and I will be there.

Respectfully,
Chaps

I was very impressed by this Sailor because he took full responsibility for his actions by actually coming by my office to apologize. That was man-sized stuff!

From: CHAPS@SHREVEPORT
To: RB@HOME

Subject: Leaving La Maddalena

Hey!

I am back in the office with a boatload of counseling. It is primarily "hangover" counseling, though. Sailors who did or said something while they were out drinking often want to deal with it the next day. Unfortunately, it is typical behavior for some sailors in a foreign country. Italy is one of the wine capitals of the world. They make and consume millions of gallons of wine a year but do it sensibly and in moderation. Wine is served at lunch and dinner almost religiously but they only consume two to three small glasses of it. We, on the other hand, seem to want to consume a whole bottle in one sitting. Our differing perspective incurs heavy consequences.

Guess what *finally* came in the mail? That's right! The package with the popcorn, pictures, news articles, and birthday card is here. Thank you and thank the Lord it was not lost or stolen. You are just so thoughtful! You know the right things to put in a care package. I was not expecting the Peanut M&Ms. I showed the package to Derby and he looked at me and said, "Dude! You are going to have to share some with me." I am reminded of the song verse, "He may not come when you want him, but he'll be there right on time." Well, your package came "right on time"! Thanks so much for your continued love and support.

Chaps

From: RB@HOME
To: CHAPS@SHREVEPORT

Re: Leaving La Maddalena

Hey!

I am glad you got the package—finally! I was worried that it was lost forever. God took care of the situation.

I spoke to Cynthia Saunders this morning. She was calling from Hampton and will be in Norfolk for the missionary meeting this weekend. We had a good talk. She and Frank are leaving Saturday morning. I told her my parents will be in town this weekend so I do not think we will be able to meet but hopefully the next time they are in town or when you return we can go down there for a visit.

On our way to mail the bills and do a commissary run.

Talk to you soon.
RB

From: CHAPS@SHREVEPORT
To: RB@HOME

Re: Leaving La Maddalena

Hey!

Praise God indeed! Thanks for taking care of the bills. We are settling back into the ship's at-sea routine. Hope you guys had a good trip at the commissary.

Love,
Chaps

We departed safely from La Maddalena with memories of great food and friendly faces. It was a good three-day break for the entire ship and the last chance at Liberty (?) for a while.

-12-

BEYOND ALBANIA
Into the inevitable and unknown

02 November 2001

S ince departing La Maddalena, the seas have remained particularly rough. The incessant pitch and roll of the ship created uneasiness that seemed to amplify the uncertainty of our schedule. Rumors swirled that our next exercise, The National Training Continuum (NTC) set in the Adriatic Sea off Albania, was going to be cancelled. If so, we would be re-routed to go through the Suez Canal which we all called, "The Ditch" and everyone knew what that meant: head straight for the North Arabian Sea to send our Marines forward into the fight.

The Keeper

Let us pray.

"I lift my eyes to the hills; where does my help come from?
My help comes from the Lord, maker of heaven and earth.[4]

---

[4] Psalm 121:1-2

The Lord is my keeper; the Lord is my shade at my right hand.
The sun shall not hurt me by day nor the moon by night.
The Lord is my keeper from this time forth and forevermore."[5]

Gracious Lord,
In all your ways,
In all your plans,
In all your purposes for our lives; you are the Keeper of our souls.

In your presence, fear must subside and worry is subdued; grief is
surrounded by comfort and doubt surrenders to faith.

O Lord, we watch and we rest with the knowledge that our tomorrow is
firmly in your grasp. Continue to keep us within your perfect care.

Amen.

03 November

From: CHAPS@SHREVEPORT
To: RB@HOME

Subject: Good Morning!

We are sailing through a storm just south of Sicily and the seas and skies are not very kind. We have at least one more day of this and then we should be in the clear.

We have begun the Uniting Through Reading Program aboard ship and there seems to be a lot of interest. I made a short video presentation that is being shown today on the ship's closed circuit TV. The video gives a short description of the program and who can participate. I am making a test video tonight.

---

[5] Psalm 121 5-8

Tell Mom and Dad I said, "Hello." Boy, are we rocking and rolling out here! Keep us in your prayers.

Love,
Chaps

1947
From: CHAPS@SHREVEPORT
To: RB@HOME

Re: Good Morning!

Hey!

Most of the crew was sea sick all day long so the ship is very quiet. I can say that now with a sense of relief because it does not affect me like it used to—praise the Lord! Derby told me on his Watch last night from 2200 to 0200 he had to excuse two of his junior officers and had some of the enlisted sailors lie down on the floor of the Pilot House to lessen the effect of the waves. Every once in a while the Lord reminds us that he is in control of the wind and the waves.

I will be praying and fasting with you for your strength and peace. Thanks for sharing your day with me. I am here and I do care.

Love,
Chaps

04 November 2001
From: CHAPS@SHREVEPORT
To: RB@HOME

Subject: Sweet Peace

Hey!

I pray you had a blessed day at worship. We had a calmer day at sea which allowed us to have a peaceful and praise-filled worship service. A lot of the crew weathered the storm last night. Now the seas are laying down nicely as we head further north.

We recorded our first videotapes for the Uniting Through Reading Program. Ten people, six sailors, and four Marines showed up and were very glad they did. I get to make my video tomorrow and then it goes straight to the mailbox. Hopefully it will reach you by Thanksgiving. I will put some familiar things in there for our son like, "H is for Hat" and "A is for "Apple." Can you think of anything else? Please let me know this evening.

I Love you very much. Take care and I'll talk to you soon.

Chaps

Smoother, settling seas

Let us pray.

Gracious Lord, we praise you for reducing the surge of the great swells we had to negotiate over the past two days. While deft ship handling helped, it was ultimately your hand that sent the storm south providing smoother, settling seas.

The storm made some suffer while others found it an opportunity for their sea legs to grow. Help us to understand that a storm, in any environment of life, is both necessary and inevitable. How else could we gain and gauge our strength? How else could we realize the finite parameters of our power? Most importantly, would we altogether ignore your presence if it were not for angry seas and foreboding skies?

Thank you, Lord, for smoother, settling seas to sail and the assurance of your presence throughout and beyond the storm.

This we pray in your Mighty Name,

Amen.

"TAPS, TAPS, LIGHTS OUT! ALL HANDS TURN TO YOUR BUNKS. MAINTAIN SILENCE ABOUT THE DECKS. TAPS!"

05 November

Our transit to Albania continued, now sailing just off the heel of the Italian peninsula. The ship's schedule was the most uncertain it had been since we left Rota. The captain was trying to get word on what would be next but no one was talking at his level or higher. Even though my schedule for this first Monday of the month was pretty clear—morning deckplate ministry, Daily Prayer Meeting at 1230, Uniting Through Reading tapings from 14-1600, OPS/INTEL Brief at 1900, and the Evening Prayer at 2155—I knew that we as a crew were just going to have to wait, trust the Lord, and take things as they came. I felt in my spirit God was calling us beyond Albania.

"TATTOO, TATTOO! LIGHTS OUT IN FIVE MINUTES! STAND BY FOR THE EVENING PRAYER."

Cover Us

Let us pray.

As we stand the watch into the deep of this dark night,
As we wait for our relief with all our fading might,
As we endure the long haul uncertain of a break in sight,
Cover us, Gracious Lord.

As we deal with private struggles and mask hidden cares,
As we take the steps to carry on despite the burdens we bare,
As we look to calm our restless soul though others are unaware,
Cover us, Gracious Lord.

As we pray for loved ones sending their affection from afar,
As we connect across the sea under the great expanse of stars,
As we desire that good fortune follow wherever they are,
Cover us, Gracious Lord.

As we hope for a better day, new life to us unfold,
As we seek the promise of your peace, worth more than precious gold,
We know your love and mercy fulfill from ages old.
Cover us, Gracious Lord.

Amen.

07 November
From: RB@HOME
To: CHAPS@SHREVEPORT

Re: Sweet Peace

I could use some advice on car maintenance. How often did you put the fuel injector cleaner in your car? Do you need a full tank of gas prior to putting it in? Or can you just add it once a week? I just wanted to know for the future.

When you get back, I think I would like to start looking for another car. I do not know what to get yet, but it does not have to be new, just a good, reliable vehicle that won't cost an arm and leg and has a good maintenance record and low mileage. Any ideas?

That is all from the home front.

Love,
RB

From: CHAPS@SHREVEPORT
To: RB@HOME

Subject: 'Got more mail today!

Thanks a million for all the sweets and treats you sent! I just got it today and all of it is greatly appreciated. I am well stocked and well-loved too. The first thing I did was lay it all out on my desk and looked at all the love and care you put into the package. I really felt special. The Crunch and Munch will not last very long and I see you were smart enough to put some more popcorn in there to replace it.

I sent something to you from Italy last Thursday and it should reach you by this weekend so keep an eye out. Another package should reach you by the following weekend and that contains the video for our son. When we pull in, I am going to mail the Christmas presents for the moms, my brothers, and their families.

Thank you also for the great Thanksgiving card! I am blessed and blessed to be married to you!

Love,
Chaps

From: CHAPS@SHREVEPORT
To: RB@HOME

Subject: Sunset off Albania

Hey!

We are conducting our next exercise a few miles off the coast of Albania. The seas are the calmest since we pulled into La Maddalena and the sunset was spectacular. It is still quite mild here despite it being the middle of November. We are about on the same latitude with Toronto, Canada, which is probably very chilly by now. The warmth probably has to do with the Adriatic Sea.

We have at least a week here and then??? We expect that by now. We are merely making this up as we go, not actually but that is how it feels sometimes.

Love you,
Chaps

Guarding Against Folly

Gracious Lord, we give you praise tonight for how well things are going aboard ship. In spite of all that is uncertain and unknown, we remain high-spirited, vigilant, and best of all cooperative and cohesive.

We find ourselves not in a rut but an orderly routine. Our schedule may seem relatively light in regard to our position, which is perfectly poised to conduct amphibious operations. Its design is for flexibility so we can move at a moment's notice.

The familiarity espoused by knowing our work may tempt us to forego paying attention to detail. Help us guard against this folly. In our business, the terminal consequence of presumption, miscalculation, and sheer negligence is an error of the worst kind.

Lord, we pray that our professionalism in and of itself would be a tireless vanguard against folly and the hardships it may incur.

Amen.

"TAPS, TAPS, LIGHTS OUT! ALL HANDS TURN TO YOUR BUNKS. MAINTAIN SILENCE ABOUT THE DECKS. TAPS!"

08 November
From: CHAPS@SHREVEPORT
To: RB@HOME

Subject: Update

We are celebrating the Marine Corps Birthday today, two days early. There is a big parade on the Flight Deck, cake cutting, and a steak and lobster dinner. Do you remember the Marine Corps Ball we used to attend in Laughlin, Nevada? That is the level of preparation they are putting into this celebration. They are even requiring those who want to observe to wear their Service Dress Blue uniforms. I wish the Navy would do the same for its birthday. I will be sure to take some photos and send them to you.

We are heading out of the area today. It looks like the training here fizzled out. I am definitely going to send the families' Christmas presents from our next port visit. They may get there a couple weeks early but they will understand. Are you spending Thanksgiving with the folks or are they bringing dinner down with them? Please tell them I said, "Hi." Continue to keep us in your prayers.

Love,
Chaps

"REVEILLE, REVEILLE! ALL HANDS HEAVE OUT! BREAKFAST FOR THE CREW."

09 November
Morning Quarters

Quarters was the way that each division on ship gathered its sailors each morning at 0700 to communicate information, have face-to-face accountability, conduct inspections, and recognize good conduct. I usually let RP1 Bates attend it, though, and then have him report back to me any pertinent information that was passed. This morning was different: I was present because I had written up RP1 Bates to receive a Navy Achievement Medal (NAM) for the work he put into the renovation of the IT2 Bishundat Computer Room and the Fireman White Library. It was meant to be a pleasant surprise for all the hard work he put into the renovation of these spaces. After the Plan-of-The-Day was read and other information passed, the Division Petty Officer called RP1 Bates to the front of the formation and read-aloud his award citation:

"DEPARTMENT OF THE NAVY
This is to certify that the Secretary of the Navy has awarded the Navy and Marine Corps Achievement Medal to Religious Program Specialist First Class (Surface Warfare) Paul Bates..."

Once the citation was read, our Division Officer (DivO) pinned the medal to his uniform and shook his hand in congratulations. He had just returned to his position in the formation when I heard, "Lieutenant Brown, front and center!" I was caught off guard but obliged the summons by our DivO, standing at attention adjacent to him. The petty officer began to read the next citation. It was for me! To my complete surprise, someone had put me in for a NAM. Wow! This moment was supposed to be for RP1 Bates.

When Quarters was concluded, both RP1 and I received congratulations from every Sailor in our division. I was still stunned yet very humbled by the whole thing. I reflected later in the day and thought it was a Proverbs 11:25 moment: "A generous man will prosper; he who refreshes others will himself be refreshed."

Mail Call

I received two care packages in the mail today. One was from my wife and the other from my in-laws. My wife's package had a videotape of our son that was so special I swore to play it for the rest of the deployment. My in-laws' package contained three VHS movies; *Dr. Doolittle, Rush Hour*, and The Gospel Choir Concert from our church. They also included Hershey's Kisses with Almonds, Peanut M&M's, and a crossword puzzle book.

I ventured down to the Mess Deck and found the big screen TV was tuned to *Good Morning America*. It was featuring the homecoming of ships from the USS ENTERPRISE Battle Group. The sailors seated nearest to the screen took glances during their lunch. *Lord willing, that will be us in four-and-a-half months!*

"TATTOO, TATTOO! LIGHTS OUT IN FIVE MINUTES! STAND BY FOR THE EVENING PRAYER."

The Secret of Encouragement

Gracious Lord, as we await a word that will alter our course and focus, there exists a tension between our present tasking and a greater objective beyond the horizon. The challenge in all of this is to stay encouraged, to keep our spirits high, and morale just the same.

133

The best way to achieve this is to be thankful—and we have so much to be thankful for. We ought to begin with the simple things like good health and strength, the faculties of our minds and dexterity of our limbs, or something as basic as understanding all that we have is each other. Day in and day out, the ability to count on our shipmates is a cherished value of shipboard life.

So we give thanks to you, O Lord. In spite of prediction and speculation, we thank you for being truth and certainty in our life. In the midst of anxiety and apprehension, we thank you for being our peace and confidence. While engaging an unpredictable path, we thank you that our lives are always in your unchanging hands.

Thank you, Lord, for who you are and all the encouragement you bring to our lives.

Amen.

11 November
From: CHAPS@SHREVEPORT
To: RB@HOME

Subject: Hope you had a great day

Hey!

How has your day gone? We had another gold star Sunday provided by the Lord. Worship service was great with about twenty-five in attendance. I spent the afternoon at prayer service, managing the Uniting Through Reading tapings, and PT with Derby. By the way, he passed his Surface Warfare Officer (SWO) Board today after studying for about two months straight. It is a major accomplishment for a naval officer. They awarded him his SWO pin today, which he gets to wear the rest of his career. It is equivalent to a pilot earning his wings. We need more SWOs like Derby aboard this ship. He is a great guy and a true friend. In fact, we have become best friends.

Today was also a day of fasting. I was interceding for Derby all day. After his board was over, he told me that he had done the same and that the Lord made the difference in the board. He was filled with wisdom he could tell was not from his own mind. I reassured him that is the way the Lord works.

Keep your eyes on the newspapers and CNN for the latest developments. I remember during the New York City crisis that you were able to tell me things we had not heard about yet. That is how it will probably be during the rest of this deployment—you will know first.

I am finishing up the evening prayer and going up to the Pilot House to deliver it. I love you all very, very much.

Chaps

Sailing South for the Suez

Gracious Lord, we seek your blessing as we sail south for the Suez Canal. There is a convergence that commences tonight where all of our skill, training, and know-how meet up with the reality of our operational tasking. Things we considered routine like relieving the Watch, changing out burner barrels, or scanning the Night Orders, take on greater significance. It counts this time. That is not to say it didn't before but only that our present situation demands we be at the top of our game all the time.

Lord, we need your strength lest we succumb to fatigue and our frail minds and bodies are devoured by its consequences. We need your peace lest we become overburdened with surmounting cares both shipboard and on the home front. We need your favor lest we are overcome by gaps in our performance that appear simply because we are human. We need your presence lest we get discouraged and our well of hope runs dry.

For the needs we are aware of and the ones we cannot predict, Lord we call on you in advance to provide for them all.

Amen.

12 November
From: CHAPS@SHREVEPORT
To: RB@HOME

Subject: Heading South

Hey!

If you have not heard by now from the papers or CNN, we are headed south to go through the Suez Canal. There is another ARG (group of ships) that is at the end of their six month deployment and we are the next one to replace them. We will be there by this time next week. Please do not worry, pray. Call my mom and let her know about the change in plans.

Otherwise, I am doing fine. We left Albania far behind and are in the process of picking up some fuel and some food storage supplies. I love you all very much.

Chaps

From: RB@HOME
To: CHAPS@SHREVEPORT

Re: Heading South

I will stay prayed up for you and the crew as you head south. There was a terrible plane crash in the borough of Queens this morning. It was an American Airlines jet headed for the Dominican Republic. It crashed four minutes after takeoff from JFK and crashed into a neighborhood. There were no survivors on the plane. Twelve homes were damaged or destroyed. It seems there was an explosion prior to the crash and the plane broke into pieces before crashing. The damage and fatalities could have been increased significantly if the plane was still in one piece upon crashing. The investigators think this one was perhaps due to mechanical failure.

No other news from this end. We are headed to Richmond this weekend, then back here on Monday and then back to Richmond on Thursday for Thanksgiving.

Continue to pray for us. Take care and be blessed.

Love Ya!
RB

From: CHAPS@SHREVEPORT
To: RB@HOME

Re: Heading South

Hey!

I heard about the plane crash in New York City but not all the details. I guess the first thing someone expected was foul play. That is too bad there were no survivors. New York, as well as the flight industry, has suffered much this year.

We are opening up the Fireman White Library today! We have three new computers with the latest software for research and entertainment. The widescreen TV on the Mess Deck fell over during heavy seas and was severely damaged. This means no Monday Night Football for the crew for a while. It will keep the library quiet, as it should be.

Take care and I will talk to you soon.

Love,
Chaps

P.S. – Email will be down for a while. Please let everyone know I am okay.

Bring Peace

Gracious Lord, we petition you to bring us peace.

Settle the sea so our transit may be done in peace. If we just remain at a certain course and speed, we can predict that the sea will flatten on its own. Our forecasting equipment tells us so. But these instruments merely track your fingerprints providing the best guess for smooth sailing.

Master of the Wind, Water, and Sky, speak peace to your creation and calm the sea surrounding us.

Settle the hearts of our loved ones with your peace. By now they are aware of our new course and tasking. For nearly two months you have kept them safe and strong and we believe that we are not imposing on your goodness to ask you to continue to do so. For the combination of news, nerves, and the unknown could overwhelm them with worry.

Ruler of the restless heart, apply your peace to our loved ones in boundless abundance so they remain strong, trusting in you.

Settle our minds through your peace. Our situation is already filled with a flurry of operational requirements and fraught with varying contingencies. We need your peace to keep our focus clear and our instincts clean. For only you have known our beginnings and endings, only you have seen how the script will play out.

Sovereign Lord of all life, show us your peace as we daily abide in your presence and seek your holy will.

Amen.

Beyond Albania, our deployment was about to receive its clarified purpose: to engage in the conflict that was not of our own choosing.

14 November

0345

"NOW SET OPSECON ONE! NOW SET OPSECON ONE! MAKE ALL REPORTS TO RADIO AT EXTENSION 7745!"

Email was now as dark as the pre-dawn sky. Our ship was queued up directly behind the USS BATAAN—at a safe distance—as we prepared to enter the Suez Canal. The WHIDBEY ISLAND was directly behind us. Our entire focus was on a safe, uneventful transit. I decided to make today a deckplate ministry day to be present around the ship. I particularly wanted to look in on 1ˢᵗ Lt Adams to see how he was doing. He was sure to have some anxious memories of SHREVEPORT's last transit. He was onboard the ship when it ran aground in the canal.

Our transit would be deliberately slow—eleven hours at eight knots—and designed to take advantage of the darkness as an added measure of Force Protection. At first light, the teal green waters of the canal as well as Egypt on the starboard side and the Sinai Peninsula on the port side came into view. The topography of both sides of the canal was similar—flat, arid desert—except the Egyptian side had activity in the form of developed infrastructure, small ferry and manned fishing boats, and vegetation such as date palm trees and agricultural plots. We also saw villages, mosques, as well as modern monoliths rising from the distant sand recalling the grandeur of ancient Egyptian wonders like the Suez Canal Bridge, whose height was sufficient to accommodate the tallest cargo ships and whose tower spires resembled geometric-chiseled granite obelisks. I did not know how far away the Nile River was from our location but one thing was certain: its presence allowed the Egyptian side of the canal to be something it could not on its own—alive.

Midday

Stifling heat now sacked the relative morning coolness and the ship was baking under a brilliant dome of sunshine. Relief from any prevailing winds was non-existent. I felt bad for the sailors and Marines on Watch outside the skin of the ship providing Force Protection. I paid them a visit to see how they were doing and if they had enough water. Then, as if to add insult to injury, small swarms of flies showed up and began to shower the ship. There were far too many of them to just swat away from our faces. It required eye, nose, and mouth protection. It was annoying to say the least and I could not miss the biblical metaphor behind their presence.

By evening, we had come to anchorage in the Great Bitter Lake. All three ships remained in the lake overnight then resumed the journey in the morning.

Transit

Gracious Lord, bless us this evening and throughout tomorrow as SHREVEPORT makes her transit of the Suez Canal. There will be many more long hours of navigation and Watch standing ahead and each moment will warrant our undivided attention.

For most, this great experience shall give way to even greater responsibility. So, please allow the best of our skills to rise to the occasion. Help us to count on you as well as count on each other. In doing so, we shall win the battle against fatigue, cruising the length of the canal on-time and on-course.

In your Strong Name we pray,

Amen.

15 November
From: CHAPS@SHREVEPORT
To: RB@HOME

Hey!

We are halfway done with our transit and are at anchor in the Great Bitter Lake region. By the time you wake up and read this we will be out of our passage and into open ocean again. The sights are spectacular! The terrain on the Egyptian side of the canal reminds me of Indio, California. They even have date palms lining the water's edge. More details to follow later with some digital photos.

Love,
Chaps

One saving grace about OPSECON One is that we could receive messages from the outside world but could not transmit a response to them. So, I continued to write my wife even though I knew whatever I sent during this time stayed in an email queue in cyberspace until the restriction was lifted. My goal was to keep an electronic record of the journey so she could get a mental picture of this experience once she received the messages.

From: CHAPS@SHREVEPORT
To: RB@HOME

Hey!

We have passed through the Suez Canal safely and have entered the Red Sea. Even though we did not go ashore, it was an awe-inspiring feeling to be in the place where most of the earliest recorded history took place. The most memorable juncture was where the Suez ended and the Red Sea began. Somewhere in this vicinity, the Israelites crossed over the sea and into the Sinai Peninsula. Later today, we will pass the region by Mount Sinai itself. I feel blessed and privileged to be experiencing all of this. I will gather some photos today and send them to you later.

Once email is turned back on, it should remain that way for the entire time we are over here. However, if you do not hear from me all of a sudden, it is probably due to operational restrictions. Keep your eye on the refrigerator magnet with the command numbers handy so you can access the CareLine. Also, I can receive email from you even when I cannot send a response.

Love,
Chaps

"NOW SET OPSECON NORMAL! NOW SET OPSECON NORMAL! MAKE ALL REPORTS TO RADIO AT EXTENSION 7745!"

Keeping Our Peace

Gracious Lord, as we steam an inexorable course for the Persian Gulf, help us to keep our peace. If we focus on the front-page headlines of our circumstances, we could easily be dissuaded to lose our cool; anxiety could get the best of us, those we consider our allies may fall out of favor.

O Lord, you are our peace and there is none like you, who can so perfectly calm the storms of our souls. Keep our hearts and minds fixed upon you before our strength is sapped or we come to our wit's end.

Help us to keep our peace tonight.

Amen.

ON STATION

Poised and positioned with a purpose

21 November 2001
0812

From: CHAPS@SHREVEPORT
To: CO@SHREVEPORT

Subject: Thanksgiving Day Ceremony (Proposal)

Sir,

Below is the proposal for the Thanksgiving Day Ceremony. I decided to keep it simple and user-friendly. The names that appear are suggestions Chaplain McDowell and I came up with. We have not formally asked these individuals but we feel they will play ball. Also, they represent the broad spectrum of diversity as Americans while giving equal attention to the blue and green sides.

THANKSGIVING DAY CEREMONY
Welcome and Invocation: Chaplain Brown
Scripture Reading: Hebrew-Ensign Rosenzweig
Historical Reading: Captain Valentine

Scripture Reading: Christian-2nd Lt James
Historical Reading: LtCol Faulkner (COT)
Scripture Reading: Muslim-Sgt Elias
Historical Reading: LT Cebrian
*Special Reading: Selected Sailor or Marine
Closing Song: "America the Beautiful"- All Crewmembers
Benediction: Chaplain McDowell

*SPECIAL READING – A ship-wide solicitation can be made for sailors and Marines to submit a short comment from the subject, "My Favorite Thanksgiving." Chaplain McDowell and I will receive and screen submissions for the best content. The winning author would then read their comment during the Special Reading portion of the ceremony. All other submissions could be randomly posted in the POD—two to three at a time—until Christmas.

The total length of the ceremony should be about thirty minutes. Please comment and edit as you deem appropriate.

Very respectfully,
Chaplain Brown

From: CO@SHREVEPORT
To: CHAPS@SHREVEPORT

Re: Thanksgiving Day Ceremony (Proposal)

Perfect! Let's get the ball rolling. Good work. Solicit aggressively for the special reading of Thanksgiving memories. I really like that idea.

CO

"*DAILY PRAYER MEETING WILL BE HELD IN SACC AT 1230.*"
During our canal transit, I received an email from a staff writer at my hometown newspaper. She heard I was forward deployed from a

friend-of-a-friend, who apparently sent her my email address. She was interested in hearing about our underway experiences and sharing them with her readers.

From: CHERYL@THECRANFORDEAGLE
To: CHAPS@SHREVEPORT

Subject: It would be my honor

Dear Lt. Brown,

I am Cheryl Hehl, a Staff Reporter from *The Cranford Eagle.* I would be honored to receive any accounts of your experiences from deployment. I was thinking of it, perhaps, as an ongoing series, "From the Front," or something like that. It would provide my readers with a connection to Operation Enduring Freedom. We all long for some way to connect with those fighting for our country, and your Cranford connection is an answer to prayers.

I believe I can do right by your story and I hope you have faith in what I truly believe is a God-given talent to write. Without any college education or formal training in journalism, I have soared as a reporter for the last twelve years. It could only be a gift from God and I recognize that in a profound way.

Have a blessed Thanksgiving and tell all the guys on your ship that the folks back home are grateful for their service and we are praying for them every day.

Sincerely,
Cheryl Hehl
Staff Reporter – The Cranford Eagle

From: CHAPS@SHREVEPORT
To: CHERYL@THECRANFORDEAGLE

Re: It would be my honor

Dear Cheryl,

Thank you for the opportunity to share my experiences with your readers. I do keep a deployment journal, which focuses on my shipboard experiences, specifically as a Navy chaplain and from Operation Enduring Freedom. I do not foresee the content being a problem to consolidate and submit to you but I welcome your thoughts on a title. May I suggest, "Enduring Freedom Journal"? Please let me know what you think.

There is a naval tradition called the "Evening Prayer at Sea." Every evening underway, the chaplain recites a prayer over the ship's intercom, called the 1MC. It is the time when the crew can pause to listen and reflect about their God, life, faith, or the day's events. If I may, I would like to conclude each submission with the evening prayer that corresponds with the events portrayed in the excerpt. Just a reminder: due to operational security, the material submitted will be past events or completed training. Disclosing present or future operational contingencies is prohibited.

Thanks again for this opportunity! May the Lord bless you!

Sincerely,
LT David R. Brown
U.S. Navy
Chaplain Corps

"TATTOO, TATTOO! LIGHTS OUT IN FIVE MINUTES! STAND BY FOR THE EVENING PRAYER."

Thanksgiving Eve

Gracious Lord, grant us a day to ponder and praise you for the blessings you brought into our lives.

Grant us a time to share our gratitude with shipmates about the decks.
Grant us a moment so special, so sweet it cannot be replicated.

Grant us a feast that nourishes the body, cheers the soul, and satisfies the spirit.
Grant us laughter and lightness of heart, beneficence, and brotherly kindness.

Grant us an opportunity to connect with loved ones in our thoughts,
daydreams, and prayers.
Grant us a heart that cherishes the sentiment of home but
also relishes this instance at sea.

Grant us new hope, new life through giving thanks to you on this
Thanksgiving Eve.

Amen.

22 November
About 0430

My Thanksgiving Day started with a knock on my hatch.

"Just a minute," I uttered, half-awake, half-asleep. I made my way through the darkness and opened the hatch.

"Sorry to bother you, Sir. But I have a Red Cross Message for you," said the Sailor at my hatch.

"Oh, Okay. Thanks." I said.

I flicked on the light switch and read the message a few moments after my eyes adjusted to the sudden brightness. It was a death notification for an immediate family member of a Sailor. *Great. Just the sort of news I hate to deliver on Thanksgiving Day—of all days! Just great!* No time to pout about it, though. I had to get dressed, track down this Sailor, and deliver the news. This was going to be a tough notification.

Just after Noon
From: CHAPS@SHREVEPORT
To: RB@HOME

Hey!

It is Thanksgiving Day over here. We do have a lot be thankful for although I had to deliver some bad news for three sailors already via AMCROSS messages.

The mood of the ship is calm but not depressed. Most are looking forward to the Flight Deck ceremony and the meal afterwards. Captain placed the ship at holiday routine, which allowed most to sleep in. However, my day began about one-and-a-half hours before Reveille trying to track down a Sailor who received an AMCROSS message about the death of an immediate family member. Then, two more messages followed later in the morning. So my day, so far, has been dedicated to grief ministry. Please pray for my strength and peace on this end.

It goes without saying that I miss you all very much and I wish I could be with you this Thanksgiving. I am thankful for last year's celebration. Do you remember how great it was to have your parents over our house? Please know my love and my prayers are with you as you travel to Richmond to celebrate. Take your time and drive carefully. I will be sure to send some photos from the ceremony.

I love you. Have a Happy Thanksgiving!
Chaps

Thanksgiving Dinner
1500

Captain ordered two special sittings in the Wardroom for the Thanksgiving dinner meal. The first sitting was for him, the department heads, the COT, and his primary staff. The XO and the junior officers, both Navy and Marine, would lead the second. I offered the Invocation grace over the meal. Chaplain McDowell did the same for the second sitting. After grace, we took our seats and were served by the food service assistants on hand.

The meal was delicious and it featured all the standards of the holiday: roasted turkey, stuffing with gravy, jellied cranberry sauce, sweet gherkins, candied yams, green beans with sliced almonds, and fresh-baked yeast rolls. We could have the beverage of our choice but there was also a special champagne glass filled with sparkling apple cider that would be used to offer toasts to the Nation, the Navy, and the Marine Corps later in the meal. Much of the conversation was lighthearted small talk with the only references to home being the upcoming pro football game between the Packers and the Lions. A few officers mentioned they enjoyed the Thanksgiving Ceremony on the Flight Deck earlier in the day.

After the meal, I chose not to head to the Wardroom Lounge to watch the football game but, rather, look in on the Sailor who had received the Red Cross message. The nature of his message warranted sending him home on Emergency Leave. Unfortunately, we were five-hundred miles from nowhere in the middle of the Gulf of Aden near Yemen and it would be another three to four days before we could even fly him off the ship.

23 November

With Thanksgiving over, the ship continued on its trek to the North Arabian Sea and eventually off the coast of Pakistan, where we would remain On Station until further notice. We were back into the open waters at the bottom of the Arabian Peninsula, sailing past Yemen and Oman. OPSECON Normal was set throughout the ship and the Force Protection Watch was ordered to stand down. I was now able to answer my email and soon the ship would return to its normal routing.

"SWEEPERS, SWEEPERS, MAN YOUR BROOMS! GIVE THE SHIP A GOOD SWEEP-DOWN BOTH FORE AND AFT. SWEEP-DOWN ALL LADDERWELLS, LADDERBACKS, AND PASSAGEWAYS! HOLD ALL TRASH AND GARBAGE ON STATION."

Our arrival in the North Arabian Sea would be a bit premature because the assets of the PELELIU ARG had not cleared out for the staging area in Pasni, Pakistan. The PELELIU, along with its sister ships, would be off the coast for the next several days embarking their Marines and support equipment. With this development, we were unofficially in the hurry-up-and-wait mode of operations. We would be soon receiving the order to cut squares until we had the green light to send our Marines ashore.

After the OPS/INTEL Brief, the captain spoke to the crew over the 1MC, first with a pat on the back for their efforts during the heightened security watches and encouragement for the ship for what would be happening in the next several days. He also encouraged the crew to step outside the ship this evening and notice the awe-inspiring sight of the stars in the Arabian night sky. I took his suggestion, stepped outside the skin of the ship, and marveled at the opaque clarity of the sky and its awesome array of stars.

Lull in Our Heart

Gracious Lord, our present posture should not be perceived as a lull in our schedule. Rather, it anticipates planned decisive action.

However, if there be a lull tonight, let it be in our hearts. Let us encounter a portion of your peace that is all our own, a solitary place in which you desire to furnish and dwell.

Open hearts about the ship as they await the sound of your voice t o provide assurance, guidance, and strength.

Speak, Lord! Create an echo in our souls that never ceases to reverberate, one that resounds with your truth and love.

This we pray in your Everlasting Name,

Amen.

"TAPS, TAPS, LIGHTS OUT! ALL HANDS TURN TO YOUR BUNKS. MAINTAIN SILENCE ABOUT THE DECKS. TAPS!"

24 November
From: CHAPS@SHREVEPORT
To: RB@HOME

Subject: Good Morning!

Hey! I hope you are enjoying those after-Thanksgiving Day sales. How early did you get up and go shopping? I wonder if the current situation has put a damper on the number of shoppers.

Well, we are finally out of our security condition and so email has been reinstated. I still cannot talk specifics but I am sure you understand. Keep watching CNN in this regard.

I am getting ready for Bible Study this evening and worship in the morning. Have a blessed day!

Love,
Chaps

Even though the ship had a good Thanksgiving, I noticed in a lot of my deckplate conversations that they missed being home. That was understandable, though. Thanksgiving is synonymous with being home and enjoying the three "Fs": family, food, and football.

I was somewhat concerned that the slowing pace of our schedule would give the crew more time to think about where they were, specifically, how far they were from everything sweet, familiar, and dear. If we keep a crew busy, their minds will stay focused on their work and one day will fold into the next. Unfortunately, giving them a pause or a gap in work may allow some sailors to become restless. In a strange way, I hoped that our schedule would pick up soon to avoid losing focus. That is when sailors get careless and then mistakes, accidents, and injuries are just around the corner.

"DAILY PRAYER MEETING WILL BE HELD IN SACC AT 1230."

Tomorrow, Preparation Sunday, will be the first Sunday in the season of Advent. I had been working all week from the prescribed scripture found in the Common Lexionary. The message would focus on the coming of Jesus, first into the world as the Messiah, then as the soon coming King of Kings. As a minister, I always enjoyed observing the seasons within the Christian calendar. Each one provided the theme and context for worship and preaching. It was also a very practical way of transmitting the gospel.

Before the evening was out, RP1 Bates came by my stateroom to give me a thumbs-up that the altar vestments, communion elements, and the Advent Wreath were all in place and ready to go.

"TATTOO, TATTOO! LIGHTS OUT IN FIVE MINUTES! STAND BY FOR THE EVENING PRAYER."

The Herculean Task

Gracious Lord, in order to uphold relationships, carry out our duties, encourage our loved ones, remain vigilant on Watch—all the while having to take care of ourselves and maintain our focus—is a Herculean Task!

As we take our initial steps into the unknown bearing the burden of these things, we are thankful we do not have to carry it alone. Lord, you are always there. At times, our emotions and pride may blind us to this truth. The fact remains that you know our load limit is not as large as we perceive and your presence picks up the slack created by our anxiety.

Lord, you are the only force in the entire universe we can comfortably surrender to, for it goes against our identity as sailors and Marines to do so. But surrender we must; it is the only acceptable exchange you provide in order for us to experience lasting peace.

Please, Lord, carry the cares and concerns that have taxed our hearts and minds and spent our strength.

This we pray in your Mighty Name,

Amen.

26 November
From: CHAPS@SHREVEPORT
To: RB@HOME

Honey,

I am sure you all enjoyed the rest of your holiday at your parents' house. I have been dreaming of turkey sandwich leftovers all weekend. To me, that is the best thing to do with turkey after Thanksgiving. Needless to say, no leftovers aboard ship but I will survive.

We are getting a new Executive Officer. He is already aboard ship and going through turnovers with all department heads. My meeting with him last night went pretty well. I do not believe he is a Christian like our departing XO but he does not seem opposed to ministry in general. After he listened to my evening prayer last night, he offered this suggestion, "Perhaps you could put a slogan at the end of your prayers, something the crew can identify with the ship. The chaplain on my previous ship did that and it was a great way to get everyone to listen to the prayer." I am going to miss our present XO. He has a strong Christian character and spiritual discernment, which made working with him a delight.

As always, keep watching CNN for the latest developments. Drive safe and have a blessed day.

Love,
Chaps

"OPS/INTEL BRIEF, WARDROOM."

The main topic for tonight's brief was the debarkation plan for the Marines, which was unofficially named, "OP-Freedom D-Day." The XOT discussed that once the Marines were ashore in Pasni, Pakistan, they would be transported to Khanduhar Airport and set up Forward Operating Base (FOB) Rhino. After that, there was a question mark.

The brief was thorough and solicited few questions concerning how the operation was going to proceed. The only problem was that, as we had been warned, we would have to wait until the ships from the PELELIU ARG were completely embarked and cleared the area. There was even a rumor that our military presence footprint at Pasni was becoming too big and all operations would slow until our presence satisfied the local officials.

The body language of some at the brief showed frustration and anxiousness, especially with the Marines. They were anxious, not only to get off the ship, but to get into the fight. Privately, I was glad for the extra time with them because once they were gone, that was it—no one knew when or how many were coming back to the ship.

OP Freedom D-Day Delay

Gracious Lord, through no fault of our own we find ourselves in a reprieve from the pre-planned night operations schedule. Should we chalk it up to an oversight onshore or are you just exercising your Sovereign will? If we consider the latter, we come across several different answers you can employ to address our situation.

They are "Yes," which we understand and welcome wholeheartedly. "No," which we understand as well but accept grudgingly. But there is one more, "Wait," which is the least understood or expected.

To wait requires patience because it stifles our anxiety, churns our emotions, frustrates our sense of control, and deflates our pride. Waiting is easier said than done.

Waiting does not suggest idleness or inactivity. Rather, it provides an opportunity to re-tool and re-think our operational posture. It also gives us another chance, Lord, to examine where we stand with you.

Lord, let us take this apostrophe in tonight's schedule to thank you and realize that to wait is as logical as "yes" or "no" and in situations like this, far more necessary.

This we pray in your Sovereign Name,

Amen.

27 November

"REVEILLE, REVEILLE! ALL HANDS HEAVE OUT!
BREAKFAST FOR THE CREW!"

0658
From: RB@HOME
To: CHAPS@SHREVEPORT

Re: Good Morning

Hey Chaps!

I hope all is well and quiet where you are. Your mom asked about you and I told her you were doing fine.

I did not get in the mad rush for Christmas shopping. I went to one store late on Friday afternoon and walked right out when I saw how long the lines were. Speaking of Christmas, what do you suggest getting for your family members? Please let me know so I can get cracking. Not much time left.

Hope to hear from you soon.

Love,
RB

It was official. The BATAAN ARG would be cutting squares until PELELIU cleared the area. Our proximity would provide a good opportunity to cross-deck with the BATAAN to meet up with the chaplains and to see how the ministry was going for them over there. The delay would present several flights a day between our ships. In order to get on one of those flights, I would have to contact the CCO and have him place me on the flight manifest then apprise the chaplains aboard BATAAN of my flight plans.

-14-

ODYSSEY

God, what's going on?

28 November 2001
0800

Today presented an open door to cross-deck with the BATAAN for about four hours. The first flight was scheduled to depart in the morning and I would return around 1300. Chief Ducass and I planned to spend a few hours visiting the chaplains, the chapel, and some of the Christians aboard the ship. As I made my way to the Flight Deck, the Combat Cargo Officer (CCO) met me.

"Sir, there has been a charge plans. You are not flying over to the BATAAN."

"Well, I am not swimming over there either," I answered glibly.

"No Sir, not at all. You are actually going there by a small boat transfer."

"Small boat? What happened to the HELO?"

"The flight got canceled so all passengers going to the BATAAN this morning will be in the RHIB (Rigid-hulled inflatable boat) Boat. Do you get sea sick?" he asked.

"Uh, well..."

"Just kidding," he said. "The seas are very calm and the trip should be no problem."

"Okay, but am I still on the manifest?"

"Yes Sir! You and Chief Ducass are scheduled for the trip this morning."

A boat ride. Hmmm. Okay. Just as long as it can get me over there safely and back...today!

"Okay. Once again, CCO: I am going over on the RHIB Boat but I am flying back in a HELO?"

"Yes Sir. You are manifested for the 1330 flight from BATAAN back to SHREVEPORT—make sure you are on it."

"Roger that!" I agreed.

The CCO also informed me that there would be about ten other passengers which included the COT and the Sergeant Major. He further instructed me that I needed to muster at Side Port 4 by 0815.

Chief Ducass and I met at the side port along with the other passengers. One by one, we descended the throw ladder into the RHIB Boat. When it was my turn, I looked across the water and noticed the BATAAN had pulled alongside our ship, perhaps just a few hundred yards off our port side. The CCO was right when he said the seas were calm and it was going to be a short trip. With all passengers embarked, the RHIB slowly pulled away from SHREVEPORT. It was interesting to see our ship from this vantage point. First, it looked a lot bigger from the surface. Then I noticed several parts of the hull were in need of a paint job and rust removal. I noticed a few crewmembers were in various places on the weather decks of the ship from the Main Deck all the way up to the Signal Bridge. As we pulled further away, a small sentiment of pride emanated from within and told me,

"That's your home for now."

When we reached the BATAAN, there was another ladder to climb all the way into their side port. Each passenger was checked by the manifest as having arrived safely. Once they were aboard, they handed their float coats to the petty officer with the manifest. There were a couple Marines that were there to greet the COT and sergeant major for the purpose of escorting them to a meeting with the MEU Commander. When it was my turn, the petty officer greeted me, checked the manifest and confirmed that I had arrived. I asked him for directions to the chaplain's office and he directed a Sailor to take us there. The chaplains and RPs were expecting us and gave us a warm welcome as well as a grand tour of their LMRC. Everything on BATAAN was bigger and better equipped than SHREVEPORT. They had chapel services space that could easily hold sixty to seventy people. They also mentioned they held the Gospel Service in the Foc'scle, which could seat at least 250 people. It was quite impressive. At the end of the tour, Chief Ducass and I split up so he could meet with another chief that he knew from the supply department. We agreed to meet again at the chapel to attend their Daily Prayer Meeting.

1145

The chaplain and I had lunch in the Wardroom, which was about the size of a moderate banquet facility. However, the quality of the food was about the same as our ship, proving that bigger is not necessarily better. Our mess specialists could definitely hang with theirs.

After the meal, the chaplain offered to take me back to the chapel so I could attend the prayer meeting. I told him I would be able to make it back on my own to which he cautioned, "If you lose your way, just ask a Sailor and they should be able to get you there." It took me a little longer than usual but I made it through the maze of ladderwells and passageways back to the chapel in plenty of time. Chief Ducass returned along with his colleague, whom he introduced and said he would be staying for the meeting as well. Several Marines and sailors trickled into the chapel and participated by sharing their testimonies, singing and reading scriptures. The RP had taken the liberty to introduce us and we gave a brief greeting on behalf of all the Christian brothers aboard our ship. At the conclusion of the meeting, Chief Ducass and I said our goodbyes and headed for the Flight Deck.

When we arrived, we approached a petty officer connected with the aircrew to confirm our names were on the manifest.

"Yes Sir, can I help you?" he asked.

"Yes. Two PAX for transfer to SHREVEPORT: LT Brown and SHC Ducass."

"Okay," he said looking over the list of names. "You said, 'LT Brown' and 'SHC Ducass', right?"

"Yes." He scanned the first page, flipped over to the next, then plainly said, "Sorry Sir. I do not see your names."

"What does that mean?" I asked with some concern.

"It means you are not manifested for this flight," he said.

"I understand but what does *that* mean?"

"It means there is no space for you on this flight. If you are not on the manifest then you are not here."

"What do you mean, I am not here? I am standing right in front of you!"

"I am sorry, Sir. If your name is not on the manifest, I cannot get you on the flight. Did you check-in with your CCO?"

"Yes, of course or we would not have attempted to come over here," I replied.

"Okay. Let me double check. Give me a moment, Sir." The petty officer walked over to the main manifest to look for our names. I became a bit apprehensive thinking that we were going to be stranded. A funny thought from this morning came to my mind, *we are definitely not swimming back to the ship.*

The chief and I shared a chuckle about "not being here" but privately wondered what was next. The petty officer confirmed that we were not on the manifest but there was a possibility we could be listed for the 1600 flight to SHREVEPORT. We both agreed to be placed on that manifest because that was our last chance to get back to the ship. We were told to report back at 1500.

We walked away somewhat bewildered. How could we have come over in the first place if we were not manifested? And how did our names disappear? Fortunately, Chief Ducass offered an optimistic view, "Well, Brother, it is more opportunity to have fellowship with the brothers and sisters over here. Thank you, Jesus!" I concurred but in the back of my mind I kept a caution flag raised to make sure we would not be one minute late for the final flight back to our ship.

1500

For a second time, the chief and I made our way up the ramp toward the passenger station adjacent to the Flight Deck. But the petty officer had no better news for us.

"Sir, I could not get you on the manifest. Tactical Control Squadron (TACRON) has strict guidelines that I have to follow. All PAX must be manifested twenty-four hours before they fly and there is no standby list. I am sorry."

"What should we do now?" I asked attempting to conceal my building frustration.

"Go see the TACRON officer-in-charge and see what he can do for you."

"Alright. Thanks."

We were stuck. I knew it and so did Chief, but I took the petty officer's recommendation anyway. TACRON turned out to be a dead end too. He suggested we go and see what the CCO could do for us regarding a flight tomorrow. Even though I had packed an overnight bag, I was not enthused about spending the night. I asked Chief Ducass if we could use his colleague's computer so I could email the XO to tell him about our predicament. I also realized that it was my turn to do the Evening Prayer so I needed to contact Chaplain McDowell and ask him if he wouldn't mind covering for me. The chief obliged and we decided to split up and meet in the Hangar Bay with the CCO after dinner.

About 1730

When we met again in the Hangar Bay, Chief Ducass' colleague met us there too along with the CCO. As they approached, the expressions on their faces looked like good news. After a brief introduction, he had this to offer:

"Sir, I think there is a way for you to get back to your ship this evening."

That is great!

"It is not a HELO flight. It is on the surface...in a LCAC."

I was excited to hear this news. The LCAC was the fastest craft on the water. It could travel as fast as speeds posted on an interstate highway. *Great! I would be back to the ship in no time. Perhaps in time to do the Evening Prayer.*

"There is only one thing," said the CCO. "You have to go the beach first."

"The beach?" I inquired in disbelief. *"AAAHH! The beach?! That is Pakistan! I had to go to Pakistan first?*

"CCO, are you sure we have to go to the beach? I mean, isn't there another way?"

"No Sir. You have to take an LCAC to the beach and then an LCU back to your ship. It is the only way you can get back this evening."

He was saying it would be a quick ride to the shore and a very, *very*, slow ride back to the ship. It could take several more hours to complete this trip, perhaps returning sometime after midnight.

"Can I put you on the manifest, Sir?"

"Sure, sign us up," I said with some dejection.

Chief Ducass and I looked at each other, shook our heads, and smiled.

"Brother, we are going to Pakistan tonight. Can you believe that?"

"All praise to the Lord, Chaplain!" Chief said laughing. "Our lives are in His hands."

God, what's going on? I thought I did everything right and I am not sure why things are not going our way.

All I could think about was that I, as a shipboard chaplain, had no business going to the shore, especially without the captain's permission.

The LCAC was scheduled to arrive in the Well Deck around 1830 to pick up some tractors and a 5-Ton truck and return to the beach. Estimated time of departure was 1930. The chief and I had some free time before we had to muster in the Well Deck for the trip but we did not dare move from our spot in the Hangar Bay. This was our only ticket back to SHREVEPORT and we were not going to miss it for anything.

The long ramp descending into the Well Deck served as the ship's smoking area during Flight Quarters. About eighty sailors and Marines, both male and female, were congregated and fully engaged in smoking and joking. The majority of them were young, perhaps nineteen to twenty-one-years-old. Apart from its addictive qualities, smoking was a social ritual for some, an opportunity to caress the habit, blow off steam, or meet new people of the opposite sex; wanting to be wanted and displaying that desire through body language and verbal cues. I observed all of this thinking, *Do they know anything about the love of Lord? Could they even fathom any kind of personal fulfillment beyond the mesmerizing grasp of flirtation and infatuation?*

1920

A chief from the Well Deck crew met us at the top of the ramp to inform us the LCAC was about to arrive. He brought with him two sets of cranial headsets and float coats and then led us down the ramp, past the smoking area, and to the top of the Well Deck. The well was already flooded due to the ship being ballasted down for amphibious operations. We could hear the approach of the LCAC while it was a quarter mile away. Its large turbofans preceded its arrival and only grew in intensity as it drew closer to the ship. Directly in front of us were a tractor, Humvee, and other large equipment that was to be embarked with us as we headed for the shore.

Guided by the Well Deck crew, the LCAC made its way cautiously into the ship. Even though the cranial gear protected my ears from the roar of its engines, I could still feel the power as it made the air and decks throughout the space reverberate. My mood began to change as I considered this trip to the beach—at least the "getting there" part—was going to be pretty exciting.

It took about fifteen minutes to embark the heavy equipment and then it was our turn. We were led down to the lip of the vessel, up the ramp, and squeezed our way to the entrance beside the crowded Main Deck. The "pilots," who were not actually aviators but dressed like ones—flight suits, gloves, headsets and all—greeted us. The crew invited me to sit in the back behind them so I could see the ride through the front windshields. There was no room for Chief, though, which was something I did not prefer. Chief did not mind, though.

The inside resembled an instrument panel from any commercial aircraft with scopes, RADAR, gauges, and dials. The cabin itself was dark and so all the readings came across in bright fluorescent green. The windows were clear and unobstructed.

Our ride to the beach was smooth and fast. Once we arrived we disembarked the LCAC along with the crew.

"Thanks for the ride!" I told them.

"No problem, Sir," they answered.

"Where is our ride back to the ship?"

"It is about one-quarter mile down the beach. Can you see its lights?"

I looked carefully and saw the lights of the LCU. It was resting near the shoreline.

"Yes. Thanks again."

The chief and I made our way down the beach with bags in tow. "Welcome to Pakistan!" I said laughing along with the chief. The sand was soft and deep making our progress slow but steady. The beach was completely dark save the chemical light sticks used to mark embark/off-load boundaries. The ambient light of the full moon helped illuminate the area.

We ambled along and met the first group of personnel. They were from the BeachMasters' unit and as a matter of security they stopped us to see who we were.

"Good evening Shipmates!" I greeted them.

"Is that you, Chaplain?"

"Yes it is."

"What the heck are you doing out here?" one Sailor inquired.

I was about to give him an explanation but pragmatism overruled. "It is a long story—don't ask."

Further down the beach, we ran into OIC for the BeachMasters. "Chaps, is that you? What the hell are you doing out here?"

"Long story, Bos'n. Don't ask."

"Hey, but I am glad you are out here. A couple of my guys need some motivation, need to see you."

"Actually Bos'n, we are just trying to get to the LCU so we can get back to the ship," I explained. The last thing I wanted to do was to engage in some seashore counseling sessions.

Continuing with our trek, we came upon a contingent of Marines. I was able to pick out the COT and the sergeant major and decided I should take a moment to greet them.

"Good evening, Sir!"

"Is that you, Chaps?!

"Yes, Sir!"

"Way to go Chaps! You came out here to motivate my Marines. Good on Ya!"

"Uh, yes Sir!" At that moment I did not have the courage to tell him I was just passing through on my way to getting a ride back to the ship so I could crash in my stateroom.

"OORAH Sir!" barked the sergeant major. "Thanks for coming out!"

"No problem, Sergeant Major."

As we drew near to the LCU, a Marine sergeant serving as our liaison met us. I noticed it was at anchor near the shoreline but not onshore. Just then, I began to piece things together. *LCACs can come completely ashore, LCUs cannot. We were Onshore; the LCU was not. Ocean water was between the LCU and us.*

"Sergeant, how are we getting out to the LCU?" I asked.

"We have to walk, Sir. But do not worry the water is warm and it is not that deep."

"Sergeant, we will all get soaked! There has *got* to be another way."

"There is room for one person in the Humvee."

"Chaplain," the chief interjected, "I will walk out to the ship. You take the Humvee."

"No Chief. I will walk. Here, take my bag with you so at least it will be dry."

We began to walk, the ocean water met my boots, then my left calf, with the first step, my right knee with the next. Each step the water increased in depth. Thankfully, the waves were small and the water was warm, just as the sergeant said. I was about ten feet from the LCU and the water seemed to reach its peak somewhere at the top of my chest. *Great! At least I did not get totally soaked.* I was just about at the lip of the LCU when one last wave came out of nowhere. I could see it was taller than I was so I decided to rise off the ocean floor to meet it. This way I would not get submerged inside the wave. I was successful at that but now I was totally soaked. The sergeant, who seemed to be slightly amused, helped me up the ramp of the LCU. My boots squished with each step on its steel deck.

"Is that the chaplain? Chaps! What the hell are you doing out here?" asked the chief of the landing craft.

"Don't ask," I replied. I was in no mood to talk at all. The crew seemed glad and surprised to see me, though. I was definitely the last person they expected to come aboard.

Shortly after I arrived, the Humvee carrying Chief Ducass made its way up the ramp and onto the vessel. The Humvee was not as waterproof as I thought. The chief was wet up to his knees. My bag on the other hand was completely dry, and again, I was thankful for that.

"Chief, when do we depart?" I asked anxiously.

"'Can't leave right now, Sir. My guys are trying to fix some problems with the engine. Why don't you go down below and grab something to eat?"

Food was the *last* thing on my mind.

Oh Lord, I just want to get back to the ship.

About Midnight

All I could think about was getting out of my soaked clothes and into the only dry clothes I had—my pajamas. I asked if they had a dryer onboard and they told me that they did. I decided to shower and stay in my robe while my uniform dried. That took about a-half-hour. I began to relax in the lounge below the Main Deck. I asked Chief Ducass if he minded if I took a nap. He did not so I did.

We received word that the engine problem had been fixed and we could be underway very soon. The LCU was much noisier below decks than our ship. I came up to the midship galley to get my uniform. It was still warm from the dryer and it was so relaxing to put it back on.

Sometime after 0200

We should have been underway but when the ship attempted to pull away, it got stuck on a sandbar. Apparently, in the time it took to repair the engine, the tide went out leaving us stranded on a sandbar. It took about another forty-five minutes to get us dislodged, turn the LCU around and head for SHREVEPORT.

I tried to get some sleep in the galley, resting my head on the tabletop. Unfortunately, the engines made the countertop vibrate and the entire side of my face was humming with the effect right through to my teeth. The rattle of the deck in the galley also did not allow me to rest.

Exhausted beyond frustration, I decided to get some air above decks. The full moon illuminated the sky and the waters ahead of the craft. SHREVEPORT was now coming into view. As the ship came closer, I began to recount the day's events seeking somehow to make sense of it all. With the Well Deck in view, I could not escape the silhouette that the ship's mast made against the full moon. It was in the form of a cross and for a moment, I did not notice the noise of the engines or the sound of the sea. It was as if I could sense the Lord saying:

I Am Your Peace

The LCU made its way into the Well Deck of the ship. Once it was secured, we debarked, said "Good night," and headed for our rooms.

It was 0415. Reveille was in less than two hours.

JASMINE

Out of the sky, she came

29 November 2001

I was heading to lunch when one of the officers stopped me in the passageway and said, "Hey Chaps! There was somebody looking for you in the Wardroom. I think she is the new PACE (Professional Adult College Education) Instructor. She just arrived today on the first HELO flight."

"Okay. Why did she ask for me?" I said.

"Well, she was wondering if we had a Bible Study on ship," she said.

"Okay. Thanks!" I said.

It is her first day on the ship and she wants to know about Bible Study. She has got to be a Christian! My curiosity was stoked as I made my way to the Wardroom to meet her.

When I entered the Wardroom, she was sitting at a table by herself going over some papers. A civilian female in this environment stuck out like a sore thumb. It looked like she had already finished her meal. Instead of greeting her right away, I decided to go grab a plate of food then join her at the table.

"Hi! May I join you?" I asked.

"Yes, please do!" she said.

I sat down and extended my hand to her saying, "I am Chaplain Brown.

Welcome Aboard!"

"Jasmine McMurphy. I am the new PACE Instructor," she said.

"Good to meet you, Jasmine."

"Good to meet you too, Chaplain."

"Someone told me that you were looking for me. Is that so?" I asked.

"Yes. I wanted to know if you had a Bible Study aboard ship," she said.

"We do. It is held in the evenings at 2000 on the Mess Deck," I said.

"Great!" she responded. "What do you all do for worship?"

"Well, we normally have Protestant Worship Service on Sunday mornings at 0900 in the First Class Petty Officer's Mess, which is on the port side of the Mess Deck."

"Terrific!" What about during the week? Do you all meet for fellowship?" she asked.

"We have a Daily Prayer Meeting that takes place at 1230 in a location called 'SACC,' which is two decks above us."

"Cool! I am looking forward to supporting your ministry on the ship," she said.

"That's great. Whatever time you have, please feel free to join us," I said.

"I will," she said smiling.

We talked for another ten minutes or so then she excused herself to go prepare for class registrations at the Admin office. She was very congenial and optimistic. After she departed, the encounter with her lingered in my mind. *Yep! Definitely a Christian.*

1230

I told the brothers at prayer meeting about Jasmine and that we could expect to see her at times here or at worship. They were glad to know there was another strong Christian aboard the ship. Chief Ducass immediately recognized how great the potential of her witness could be among the sailors in her classes.

The PACE program offered opportunities for working adults to earn a college degree. The Navy used PACE Instructors to provide such opportunities for its sailors through teaching accredited college courses aboard ships that were forward deployed. There were specific colleges that sponsored and trained these instructors for the purpose of conducting courses aboard ships. Anyway you looked at it, the presence of PACE Instructors was a winning proposition: sailors got started or continued their college education, the Navy got a smarter workforce and higher retention rate, the college increased its business and gained name recognition among sailors that could be brand-loyal students whether they stayed on Active Duty or not.

"SWEEPERS, SWEEPERS, MAN YOUR BROOMS! GIVE THE SHIP A GOOD SWEEPDOWN BOTH FORE AND AFT! SWEEP DOWN ALL LADDERWELLS, LADDERBACKS, AND PASSAGEWAYS! HOLD ALL TRASH AND GARBAGE ON STATION!"

From: RB@HOME
To: CHAPS@SHREVEPORT

Subject: Car Maintenance

Mission Accomplished! I went to Firestone today and they worked on the car for two-and-a-half hours. According to them, you do not need the spark replaced until 96,000 miles. This is according to their vehicle maintenance schedule. They also showed me that this information is located under the hood of the car. So, you have a while before replacing them.

Ironically, the Check Engine light came on again on my way to Firestone, so I had them do the fuel system cleaning to be on the safe side as well as transmission and coolant flush. The only thing left to do is rotate and balance the tires at 61,000 miles and check the brakes.

Tonight at dinner, our son had a small mashed sweet potato and I added some cut-up chicken and mixed it with the potato. He ate the whole thing along with some string beans and applesauce. He finished with graham crackers and strawberry yogurt. He has a good appetite.

Talk to you later!

Love,
RB

My wife had an acquired knack for car maintenance. She took care of both of our vehicles during our first deployment, covering oil changes, tire rotations, coolant flush-and-fills, etc. So I was encouraged by her business as usual message about the car.

Litany of Supplication

Let us pray.

The shifting sand of our tasking breeds impatience in our hearts.

O Lord, let your peace be the focus of our lives. May we experience contentment in our souls, so solid and secure that it mitigates all anxiety.

The multiplying concern for family and loved ones has plagued our minds with worry.

O Lord, may our confidence and trust be in your unchanging hand. May we, with bold faith, be assured that you are in control of all that is dear to us so far away.

We are tired and taxed by our schedule and fatigue has become too familiar.

O Lord, provide new strength to we who are weary. May those who stand Watch receive their second wind, those poised to relieve them grasp firmly the baton, and those at rest rejuvenated.

In your Merciful Name we pray,

Amen.

"TAPS, TAPS, LIGHTS OUT! ALL HANDS TURN TO YOUR BUNKS. MAINTAIN SILENCE ABOUT THE DECKS! TAPS!"

30 November
From: CHAPS@SHREVEPORT
To: RB@HOME

Re: Car Maintenance

Bravo! Bravo! Supermom strikes again!

Praise God for all you accomplished at Firestone! Our car probably wants to give you a kiss. Great job! I did not realize we could wait until 96,000 miles on the spark plugs. The maintenance manual says 60,000 but I am glad they pointed out otherwise. If the brakes start to feel loose or squeal, have them checked out.

I got the video you made in the mail! Our son has progressed so much in one month. He looks like he has gained some weight too.

5THINGS

God's grace and mercy in our lives
God's abundant blessings
The doors the Lord opens
Our family, our marriage
Our love

Have a blessed day and write back when you can.

Chaps

"DAILY PRAYER MEETING WILL BE HELD IN SACC AT 1230."

Jasmine joined us today at the prayer meeting and she fit right in. She did not seem uncomfortable in our all-male setting and we were refreshed by her presence. She came up with ideas no one else thought about, she sang in keys too high for us men to reach, and offered prayer requests that got right to the heart of the matter. It seemed she was going to make this midday experience an even more kind and comfortable one just by showing up.

Permanent Change of Station (PCS) Orders: RP1 Bates

It was time for RP1 Bates to leave the ship. He had received PCS orders to the Naval Amphibious Base in Little Creek, Virginia, which read, "Detach no earlier than 01 December and report no later than 31 December." His absence was going to create a gap in his position because there was not a scheduled replacement for him in the near future. From an operational perspective, the Navy did not care where sailors were in the world. When it was time for a Sailor to leave, they pulled him like a bad tooth and found a way to get him to his next duty station. In contrast, the Marines would never pull one of theirs in the middle of a deployment.

It was the most inopportune time for him to go. We had just broken the surface on the Advent Season, one of the busiest times for Christians next to Holy Week from Palm Sunday to Easter. His absence meant that I had to petition for volunteers from among the crew to fill in the certain gaps in administration and logistics. I reasoned that the first place to look was among the worshipping community itself. Then I thought, no matter how sincere the volunteers, there was going to be a drop in the quality and consistency of the support simply because they were not an RP.

"THE OPERATIONS AND INTELLIGENCE BRIEF WILL BE HELD IN THE WARDROOM AT 1900."

Tonight's brief introduced the inevitable: sending the Marines ashore and into the fight. Even though their departure was about a week-and-a-half away, every aspect of the sea, land, and airlift of forces into Afghanistan took center stage. At first, I marveled at the immense coordination and collaboration of our Blue/Green team to execute this future task. I also began to think about how hard we had worked as a crew just to get the ship all the way over to this side of the earth, yet, the most challenging work was still ahead of us. I had one thing in mind for the Evening Prayer but God changed the subject towards the end of the brief.

For the sailors and Marines

Let us pray

Lord, we offer this prayer for Sailors and Marines:

A petition for the men and women who have always said "Yes" to our nation's bidding even before she came into existence. Reward our willingness to serve and sacrifice with your blessing and favor.

An intercession for members whose mission is inextricably linked and whose heritage and history go hand in hand, extend a band of protection around all we do on behalf of our country.

A supplication for the support system on the home front that allows us to maintain focus, touch them with your love. May it bountifully reciprocate in the affection connection directed toward us.

A vesper for a breed too proud to quit, too dedicated to get discouraged, and too resilient to stay down. Grant alertness for the Watch and rest for the weary so that the continuum of vigilance may never be compromised.

Amen.

02 December

"REVEILLE, REVEILLE! ALL HANDS HEAVE OUT! BREAKFAST FOR THE CREW!"

Morning Worship

It was Jasmine's first worship service at sea. She arrived early, sat up front, and was an eager participant. After the service, she shared her excitement about preparing for Christmas and shared many ideas that she believed would get the crew more focused on the holiday.

"I think we should form a choir and sing Christmas songs for the sailors," she said.

"You think so?" I said.

"Yes! We sing really well at the Daily Prayer Meeting. It would be easy to make up a choir from there. What do you think?" she asked.

"Well, let me think about it," I said. "And I will get back to you."

"Okay. Hey! We could even make an announcement at Sunday morning worship service. There are a few sailors there who can sing too," she said.

"Okay. I will look into it," I said.

"Thanks Chaplain!"

In my mind, there was more to this than just putting together a choir. However, I did not want to squelch her enthusiasm or idealism.

It was the final rigging for a worship service at sea for RP1 Bates. He was scheduled to depart the ship later today. During the service, I acknowledged his presence in the back of the room and encouraged our congregation to say "goodbye" once the service was done. I really appreciated all he had done for me on personal and professional levels, like showing me the ropes of shipboard life, helping me get through the disaster that was my first worship service at sea, assisting with renovating the White Library and the Bishundat Computer Room, and supporting the COMREL projects in New York. I was going to miss him. He was a good Sailor and RP.

"FLIGHT QUARTERS! FLIGHT QUARTERS! ALL HANDS MAN YOUR FLIGHT QUARTERS STATIONS! WEAR NO COVERS TOPSIDE, THROW NO ARTICLES OVER THE SIDE! ALL HANDS NOT INVOLVED WITH FLIGHT QUARTERS STAND CLEAR OF THE FLIGHT DECK, HANGAR BAY AND WEATHER DECKS!"

About 1500

I met up with RP1 Bates in the Hangar Bay. He was with a group of sailors who were flying off the ship as well. They all wore their flight cranial headgear with eye and ear protection and float coats. They were queued up in a single file line toward the exit of the hangar awaiting the signal from the Combat Cargo Assistant to board the HELO.

"Alright. RP1, take care of yourself," I said loudly, speaking over the noise of the rotors.

"I will, Sir," he shouted back.

"Thanks for all you have done. I truly appreciated all your hard work," I said.

"You are welcome, Sir."

"I will have to come over to Little Creek to look you up once I get back," I said.

"Yes, Sir. Please do. Come over anytime," he said.

The Combat Cargo Assistant gave the signal that it was time to board the HELO. I gave RP1 a final handshake and pat on the back. He followed the sailors ahead of him in the line out of the hangar, onto the Flight Deck, and out to the back entrance of the HELO. *"GREEN DECK!"* came the announcement over the 5MC from the primary flight tower. With the hatch to the HELO closed, the chocks around its wheels were removed as were the chains securing it to the Flight Deck. The pilot followed the hand signals of the aviation boatswain's mate, lifting the HELO off the deck and into the sky. I was glad for RP1. He was headed home. Unfortunately, now I had to continue with the Religious Ministry without RP support, perhaps for the remainder of the deployment.

"TATTOO, TATTOO! LIGHTS OUT IN FIVE MINUTES!
STAND BY FOR THE EVENING PRAYER!"

The Name of the Lord is to be Praised

"From the rising of the sun to the place where it sets, the name of the Lord is to be praised."(Psalm 113:3)

Lord, was there any part of this day that you did not have us on your mind?

Was it during the course of the night when the Engineers got the EVAP back up and running? Was it before Reveille when the cooks and FSAs collaborated to serve brunch? Or was it at dawn when you allowed the Watch to expend their last bit of strength before they were relieved? Did you lose track of us this afternoon when the HELOs departed or forgot about us this evening during Well Deck operations?

Just the ability to answer tonight is both testimony and testament to your abundant goodness towards us. It confirms the Word already recited: "From the rising of the sun to the place where it sets, the name of the Lord is to be praised."

Amen.

03 December
0947

From: CHAPS@SHREVEPORT
To: CHERYL@THECRANFORDEAGLE

Subject: "Enduring Freedom Journal" (First submission)

Dear Cheryl,

Attached is my first submission for the "Enduring Freedom Journal." I was not sure about the length you wanted but I tried to trim and polish it the best I could. I would like to request that you keep the prayer intact. As I mentioned in the article, the Lord placed those words on my heart and I would appreciate it if you could keep them as they are. My hope is that this series would inspire as well as inform. Please respond when you can with your comments.

Sincerely,
Chaplain Brown

My first input to the hometown paper. I was anxious to hear from Cheryl on how it was being received by the readers, which probably would not happen until Christmas. This was a terrific opportunity to share my experiences and I was grateful for the exposure.

From: RB@HOME
To: CHAPS@SHREVEPORT

Subject: (No Subject)

Hey!

How were Sunday services? We went to the local service. Everyone asked about you and when you will be coming home. Our son was his usual self—tantrums at the beginning of the service, asleep by the end of it.

Oh! I found him a neat little gift at the Navy Exchange. It is an artificial aquarium with artificial fish and plants. It even has lights and bubbles. It has all the makings of a real aquarium without the mess. I think he will like it.

All is well on this side of the world. Take care and email when you can.

Love,
RB

From: CHAPS@SHREVEPORT
To: RB@HOME

Re: No subject

Sunday service was a blessing! It was the first Sunday of Advent and we celebrated it to the hilt! We even had an Advent Wreath with candles. It was so sacred.

We have begun our Holiday Support Plan aboard ship. It is a conglomeration of events that will culminate on New Year's Eve with a Watch Night service. I have to work a little harder though, because RP1 Bates has PCS-ed. It was his scheduled time to go but his departure has created more work for me. Please pray that the promised replacement will show up soon.

Have a blessed day!

Love,
Chaps

"DAILY PRAYER MEETING WILL BE HELD IN SACC AT 1230."

Jasmine's classes started this week. She taught English Literature and Business Communications to about forty sailors. I knew I owed her an answer about her Christmas Choir idea but I figured I had a few weeks to get back to her. Any way I looked at it, her presence aboard ship was a breath of fresh air. She was a civilian and a female, she could think outside the box, she was a Christian, and the best of her ideas and energy would be in support of the ministry aboard ship and the Kingdom of God at-large.

A Sweet, Serene Peace

Gracious Lord, in the calm of this evening we search for a sweet serene peace. Not as an afterthought or obligation, but a willing sojourn that takes us into the still sanctuary of your presence. Somewhere, there ought to be a part of our life and portion of our day that is reserved just for you.

For you never meant for us to be stranded by worry or meander in disillusionment or become impeded by loneliness. We were created to thrive and flourish in that environment of personal peace. It is where you remind us that we are never alone in this life; we are loved, we are special, and possess great value in your sight.

Lord, please take us to that place. Disclose its location in the heart. Lead us there if we have lost the way.

Amen.

-16-

NIGHT RAID

First mission of the war

05 December 2001

1245

We had just finished the Daily Prayer Meeting when an announcement came over the 1MC:

"ASSEMBLE ALL DEPARTMENT HEADS IN THE CAPTAIN'S CABIN AT 1300."

That is all the notice we had prior to receiving our first mission of the war. We assembled in the captain's cabin, all of the principal staff officers and the Marine Commander-of-Troops (COT). The captain kicked off the briefing by telling us the ship had been pulled from cutting Gator Squares and sent to take on a live objective. It would place the crew in direct confrontation with a probable enemy and there were a host of unknowns that made the mission particularly dangerous. It was going to be a raid executed in the relative stealth of darkness. Since it was scheduled to begin at 0300, I immediately knew it was going to be an extremely early day for the entire ship. It meant hitting the rack right after the evening prayer and getting up just a couple of hours later. Captain gave one last check around the room.

"1ST Lieutenant?"

"Good to go, Sir!"

"CHENG?"

"Ready, Sir!"

"C-O-T?"

"'Marines are ready, Sir!"

"DOC?"

"We will be ready, Sir!"

"Chaplain?"

"Yes, Sir!"

"AIR BOSS?"

"Yes, Sir!"

"Okay. Let's do this. I would like to see the C-O-T, OPS, 1ST Lieutenant, and AIR BOSS after the meeting. Any 'Oh, by the way's?'" Seeing none, the captain adjourned the meeting.

As I walked out of his cabin and headed down the passageway for my stateroom, I began to realize the gravity of the moment; there could be conflict, people could get seriously wounded, or die. I had to pray for God's peace and mercy to be on the ship but especially to those who could be heading into harm's way. After the prayer, I tried to get one last email off to my wife before the ship went into OPSECON One. Just as I reached my stateroom I heard over the 1MC:

"NOW SET OPSECON ONE! NOW SET OPSECON ONE! MAKE ALL REPORTS TO RADIO AT EXTENSION 7745!"

Too late; we had already gone dark. Perhaps my wife will figure out that I am unable to write.

2155
Pilot House

"TATTOO, TATTOO! LIGHTS OUT IN FIVE MINUTES! STAND BY FOR THE EVENING PRAYER."

Night Raid at Sea

Let us pray.

Lord, to carry out the mission at hand will require a synthesis of all elements shipboard and expeditionary. In order to be successful, we must be as sharp and as motivated as possible.

The scene is now live; there are no pause or rewind buttons, no instant replay, or training time-outs. We have done all we can to prepare. Now help us to do it right.

Protect the sailors and Marines that will be involved in tonight's mission. Settle their hearts with your peace, their minds and bodies with alertness and strength, and their faith fully intact and firmly placed in you.

This we pray in your Mighty Name,

Amen.

After the prayer, I took a shower and hit the rack.

06 December
0100

I was awakened by my alarm. I got dressed, prayed a prayer of consecration, and applied olive oil to my hands and face, commencing a long day of fasting and prayer. I headed down to the Mess Deck where all the action was going to take place. It was filled with Marines; most were lying down on their backs resting or asleep on the port side of the deck. They were in their Deuce Gear and Flak Jackets awaiting the call to board the HELOs and fly out to the objective. I walked past them, aft toward the hatch that led to the Flight Deck. The platoon commanders were there with other staff non-commissioned officers (SNCOs) discussing last minute preparations. I did my best to stay out of the way because the entire area was bristling with activity. The Marines who were resting had their helmets to their right sides and their M-16 rifles to their left. The butts of the rifles were against the floor making the weapon stand perpendicular to the deck.

As the sailors passed by the Marines on the starboard side, some paused, stared, and pointed. Perhaps they wondered how they could be sleeping on the hard, unforgiving surface of the Mess Deck. I was not surprised because I knew that a Marine could sleep anywhere. I had seen them sleep on the flat, arid expanses of the Mojave Desert, in the mountainous border region between California and Mexico, and the dense, humid jungles of Okinawa. Marines could sleep anywhere because they had been trained to fight anywhere.

The Medical Department began to set up their Triage Unit adjacent to the rows of Marines. The long tables that the crew ate their meals upon would serve as the triage beds. Luckily, the Marines were oblivious to the whole process. I was glad about that because if they noticed what the doctors and corpsman were doing they would have made the connection that this entire unit was being set up for them in the event of any casualties. The Medical Officer huddled the corpsmen together and began to brief the procedures for caring for different types of wounds and injuries. He spoke of lacerations, sucking chest wounds, burns, maiming, those who would be Walking Wounded, Emergent, or Expectant (near death). He spoke loudly in order to have his voice project over the commotion of the Mess Deck. When they were finished, they had set up about eight tables complete with IVs, bandages, blankets, etc. I prayed silently.

Lord Jesus, we need your protection over these Marines tonight.
Be with them and bless them I pray. Amen.

I thought about all the families back home who knew nothing about what their Marine was about to do and how hazardous it was going to be. Should something go wrong, the very next word they would hear would be from a Marine Casualty Assistance Call Officer accompanied by a chaplain at their front door. The family would have gone from hearing that all was okay on the last phone call or email straight into the terrible shock of the notification.

I kept going around the Mess Deck being present and visible should any need assistance. I felt a great need to talk, to share some encouraging words but the Holy Spirit restrained me. I struggled with my need to say something and the practical reality of not knowing what to say. What words work at a moment like this? I left the Mess Deck and headed for the Flight Deck to see how others were doing. I made my way through the HELO hanger to the low-level lighting of the Flight Deck. It was still quite warm outside, perhaps in the mid-eighties. I did not even get to the end of the hanger when I heard the whistling stir of the first HELO's engine. When the rotor blades began to rotate, I knew I could not stay and talk with the aircrews. The mission was about to begin and my place was back on the Mess Deck with the Marines. The second and third HELOs followed suit and would soon transport the Marines through the night to the objective.

When I returned to the aft passageway, the Marines were all on their feet lined up in a single file undulation that covered half of the Mess Deck. They were stacked and packed with their helmets and gear strapped tightly to their bodies. It was so crowded that I moved to the side hatch adjacent to the passageway and took up a visible, unobstructed position. With the HELOs now ready to fly, it would not be much longer until they got the go ahead signal. My emotions moved me to announce a prayer but once again the Spirit said, *keep quiet*. So I did. Against my own need and better judg ment, I stood in the hatchway looking and listening to the Marines. If they were stressed I would not have known it. I caught pieces of their conversa- tions; some spoke of the dinner menu this evening while others bragged of what the rest of the day would look like once they returned. I suspected everyone knew I was there but no one acknowledged my presence or asked for prayer or a word. Captain Freeman, the officer-in-charge of the Battalion Landing Team, made some small talk but was far too focused on making sure his Marines were ready to go. His platoon commanders and SNCOs were attending the specifics.

Then came the green light. The first serial walked past my position, one- by-one fully loaded with M16 rifles and gear, through the hatch that lead to the Flight Deck. *Keep quiet*, I remembered and by this time it made practical sense too. I did not want to jinx them in any way or cause them to lose their focus. Besides, technically, they were not even my Marines. Their chaplain was far away on the WHIDBEY ISLAND and simply unaware of this mission. However, at that moment in my heart, they were *my* Marines. There was a brief pause in the procession at the end of the first serial. The second serial of Marines waited for the go ahead to board the second HELO, which would come shortly after the first departed; the third serial followed suit.

I followed a few feet behind the last Marine in the third serial right up to the entrance of the hatch. I peered out into the darkness to watch them board the HELO. Once aboard, the call came from PRYFLY (Flight Tower), *"GREEN DECK!"* When the last HELO lifted vertically and found its way off into the darkness, I knew that for now my work was done.

0405

I stopped by the Wardroom to get a glass of orange juice to keep hydrated while I fasted. A couple of officers were eating breakfast but I asked to join them only for the purpose of grabbing a glass of juice and departing.

I went back to my stateroom to catch up on some sleep. It would be three or four hours before we knew how things went. Everyone aboard ship had done all they could to see that we were in the best position to send the Marines to the objective. The rest was up to the Lord.

0745

With daybreak, the first reports about the mission were streaming in: no loss of life, no casualties. Hearing this made me grateful to God and I went up to the Pilot House to see if I could get any more details from the Officer-of-the-Deck. I learned it would be another five to six hours before the Marines finished their work and headed back to the ship. Still, there were many sailors on the weather decks scanning the horizon for the first sight of the HELOs.

By now, the good news had spread throughout the ship and when the believers met for the Daily Prayer Meeting, we openly praised God.

About 1500

The first HELO made its way back to the ship ferrying the first serial of Marines. They debarked—stacked and packed—walking across the Flight Deck and into the HELO Hangar.

"Welcome back!" I shouted to the first few Marines over the noise of the helicopter rotors. "Welcome Back, Shipmates!"

"OOHRAH Sir!" several shouted in reply.

I made my way out of the hanger and back to the Mess Deck. It was good to see them return without a scratch and to know that the others were on their way.

"NOW SET OPSECON NORMAL! NOW SET OPSECON NORMAL! MAKE ALL REPORTS TO RADIO AT EXTENSION 7745."

Email was back up. I took a moment to head downstairs to check my account. There were several messages from my wife and I was relieved to see them. The messages meant she understood the silence and remembered what happens when we go dark. There were other messages as well from the pastor of Bethel AME Church in Baton Rouge, Louisiana as well as Chaplain Jennings Harrison on the USS KITTY HAWK (CV-63).

1850

The Wardroom: OPS/INTEL Brief

The atmosphere in the Wardroom was buzzing with excitement. All the Marines and sailors assembled knew that everything had gone as well as it could.

"Attention on Deck!" a Sailor announced as the captain opened the door. The entire room snapped to their feet and came to Attention.

"Carry on! Please, sit down," he said as he took his seat at the head table.

This evening's brief was long because there was a full debriefing of the mission as well as an Underway and Vertical Replenishment (UNREP/ VERTREP) Brief. Afterwards, the captain gave a good fireside speech to the entire crew over the 1MC and thanked them for their teamwork, which paid off in a successful mission. Although he told the crew to give themselves a pat on the back, he reminded them that they needed to keep their heads on straight and stay focused for tomorrow's UNREP/VERTREP.

Later that evening, Captain Freeman caught up with me and thanked me for being there at the start of the mission.

"Your presence was not lost among the Marines," he said.

A staff sergeant made a similar comment to me on the Mess Deck.

Hmmm. Keep quiet now made all the sense in the world.

Thank you, Lord! Thank you!

-17-

MALAISE

Coping with "The Point of No Return"

Distance. Distance is the operating paradigm behind a deployment. Distance made us measure time differently and treasure what we loved more discreetly. We were at the apogee of our deployment, the furthest point from home by calendar—nearing ninety days—and by location—nine thousand miles away. Sailors knew it as "The Point of No Return," the natural and quite necessary emotional detachment that occurs in the middle of the deployment cycle—and everyone was feeling it. Absence may make the heart grow fonder but distance can make it go numb—a good numb, though, one that kept us steady on course, focused on our work, and safe. In a peculiar way, distance had its own means of helping us cope with being so far away from home.

07 December 2001
Pearl Harbor Day

I happened to catch some of the live coverage of the Pearl Harbor Commemoration Ceremony in Hawaii on the big screen TV on the Mess Deck. The Chief of Naval Operations was speaking to an open-air crowd of military, civilian, and Pearl Harbor survivors, who had special seating in the front of the audience. This year's ceremony had an inescapable history-repeating-itself sentiment to it. Here we were, sixty years later, recovering from an insidious attack on our country, fully engaged in a conflict we did not start. I suppose we were so preoccupied with our present operations that no one officially made note or reference to today's significance—not in the POD or from the captain on the 1MC. However, if history was repeating itself, I thought it important to first, make note of it and second, reason that our operations ashore could be reckoned as our "Doolittle Raid," except with a much bigger punch.

"TATTOO, TATTOO! LIGHTS OUT IN FIVE MINUTES! STAND BY FOR THE EVENING PRAYER."

An Incredible Week

Let us pray.

Gracious Lord, we take a moment this evening to reflect on how you have blessed us throughout this week. Our week began with the ship carrying out its usual tasking; repetitious Gator Squares that seemed to cut invisible grooves in the ocean. The heroics of restoring the EVAP gave way to the ensuing euphoria of the Steel Beach Picnic. Then, we were plunged so suddenly and swiftly into executing the Night Raid. And the work continues with tomorrow's UNREP and VERTREP. In short, it has been an incredible week at sea.

Lord, wherever it has left us depleted, please replenish us.
Whatever lingering tension or anxieties it has created, please relieve us.
If it has left an empty feeling or more specifically, deepened our need for you, fulfill us and satisfy all our desires according to your will.

This we pray in your Holy Name,

Amen.

08 December

My counseling load began to pick up and I saw a familiar pattern: married sailors on their first deployment who were concerned or anxious about the change in the frequency of email from their wives. Throughout the journey, they enjoyed numerous daily messages from home but they dwindled to just one message a day or every other day. Their suspicions ranged from falling out of love to flat-out infidelity.

I had experienced this very same thing when I was on deployment with Marines in Okinawa. When the emails dropped off in the middle of the deployment, they thought the worst. Back then, I created a program called the Mid-Deployment Marriage Seminar to address the problem. The seminar walked the Marines through the emotional stages of a deployment and how it affected communication between a husband and wife. I taught the Marines that the diminishing email communication signaled their spouse was becoming more self-reliant—washing clothes and cars, cleaning bedrooms and babies' bottoms, paying bills and picking up toys, daily drop-offs and pick-ups at schools and day care. At this point of the deployment, spouses have learned to do it all on their own. They have even formed a new emotional support network upon which they rely. Hence, the dwindling number emails from the home front.

All I had to do to update the seminar was to change some of the language from "green" and make it "blue" for the sailors, and then provide a brief for the captain. I was also going to wait until the numbers reached ten or more before I started.

"FLIGHT QUARTERS! FLIGHT QUARTERS! ALL HANDS MAN YOUR FLIGHT QUARTERS STATIONS! WEAR NO COVERS TOPSIDE, THROW NO ARTICLES OVER THE SIDE! ALL HANDS NOT INVOLVED WITH FLIGHT QUARTERS STAND CLEAR OF THE FLIGHT DECK, HANGAR BAY AND WEATHER DECKS!"

A huge mail drop! It was the biggest one we had since departing Norfolk. So much mail that there was not enough space in the post office to store it.

The bulk of it was "Any Sailor" anonymous mail, which consisted of letters, greeting cards, and care packages from all over America. I offered up the ship's library as a temporary storage place for scores of boxes of mail until the ship set up some sort of distribution plan.

Once the boxes of anonymous mail were stacked neatly in the front corner of the library, I randomly picked one of the smaller ones and opened it up. It contained literally hundreds of letters and cards from all across the country. I began to do the math as I scanned all the other boxes. *Wow! There must be eight to ten thousand letters in all.*

I went back to the stack and picked out another box, a larger one whose dimensions were about eighteen by twenty-four inches. When I opened it, I was surprised by what I found: two large, hardback photo albums—one plain dark blue, the other patriotically red-white-blue adorned—each with a label that read, "WE STAND TOGETHER: Messages of Support and Appreciation for our Armed Forces." I opened the blue one expecting to see photos and to my surprise I found it filled with hand written letters and notes in pen and black marker. On the inside cover was a Preface page. A veteran's group had partnered with a national department store chain to produce a chronicle of support for the U.S. Armed Forces directly from the American people. What they had produced were these album documents filled with notes of appreciation to encourage and inspire military personnel.

There were messages from Grove, Oklahoma...

WE STAND

TOGETHER

MESSAGES OF SUPPORT AND APPRECIATION FOR OUR ARMED FORCES

Stay strong, remember what you're fighting for—our freedom! God bless America!
—A. W.

I'm thankful for the men & women of the USA military forces. My prayers are with you all. Remember the words of Psalm 91: "He that dwelleth in the secret place of the Most High shall abide under the shadow of the Almighty. And I will say of the Lord, 'He is my refuge and my fortress, my God—in him will I trust.'" It goes on to say that no destruction, plague or evil can come near those who trust in God and he gives his angels charge over you. This is my prayer for our military & our Nation. —T.

Our prayers are with you. Thanks for everything you have done for our country. God bless each & every one of you. God is watching over you. We pray each and every one of you come home safely. God bless America! Love,
Missy, Shelby, & Erin

Thank you for fighting for our country. We are proud of you! —Chase R.
Age 7

Our prayers are with you daily. May God bless your efforts! We love each of you! —Chase's Mom

Thank you for giving of yourselves to our country. May God bless & keep you safe for all you do now in our time of need. Sincerely,
Gary B.

Godspeed to all who defend our nation! May you succeed and let justice prevail! Thanks for your courage—everyone return home "safe." Our flags are flying. —P. B. J.

Our thoughts and prayers are with you; and just remember you have a whole nation united behind you. May you come home safe and sound! God bless,
K. Johnson

To the ones that read this and to the ones who don't get the chance to—Thank You! No matter how big or small your job, there are no small heroes. For we at home only know that we are blessed to have you over there for us. This nation loves you. Be proud, be careful, and come back to us. God loves you and so do we. —John E. & Jordan J.

God bless all of you out there. We pray for your protection and guidance every day. Thank you for defending a belief, a people, a Nation, and God. You are forever in our prayers. God bless the USA and all she stands for. Amen.

—*Mary B. & Family*

We thank you for always being ready to defend our freedom. Thank you for your courage, stamina, and pride in the American way of life! May God keep you safe and give you strength, clear thoughts, and steady hands.

Our love & prayers,
Pat & Gayle E.

...and from Plano, Texas:

WE STAND

TOGETHER

**MESSAGES OF SUPPORT AND APPRECIATION
FOR OUR ARMED FORCES**

The big heart of Texas is with you. There's not a day that goes by that we don't think about NYC. Please be strong—we are still with you!

No more patriotic person ever lived than my father, W. H. Speller. Long before I knew why, I knew we lived in the greatest country on earth because Daddy said so. He would feel so proud of each of you, and I feel that pride too, which he instilled in me. His <u>was</u> the greatest generation—but not the last one to love our country and be willing to fight for it. God bless you all! —*S. S. Davies*

We think you are awesome!!! You are in our daily prayers.

Thank you for your courage, bravery, intelligence, knowledge, concern, and caring. You are <u>wonderful!</u> Please be careful and come back home to us safely.

Thank you for standing for what is right...sometimes it's hard to do the right thing when it seems that people who are innocent become the victims of unrighteous acts. You should be very proud of protecting freedom just as we are proud of you. United we stand for good...United we stand for freedom...United we stand in prayer for righteousness to overcome the evils of terrorism.

Dear Soldiers, Sons & Daughters,

My prayers are for you. We are so thankful for you. God will see you through. Words can never express my gratitude for all the effort in defending our great USA.

Love & Blessings,
G. Dane

P.S. – I was in the WAVES (U.S. Naval Reserve—Women's Reserve) in the 1950's.

Thank you for keeping our country safe. I hope all of you will win. Come back soon. I live in Plano, Texas. I am six years old.   *—P. W.*

May God give you comfort as you are separated from your family and loved ones. Remember to pray—please renew and strengthen your faith in the Lord by reading the Bible! Jesus loves you!

Being a naturalized citizen of this great country America—I truly appreciated all the opportunities and freedom that this country offers me. I know without a shadow of a doubt I "owed it all to you all!" Keep up the good work. We are so proud of you all. We will continue to pray for you and all your loved ones. God bless you all!   *—C. M. Lum*

I think the people who have the guts to go and save other people are very nice.

—K. G. R.
Age: 7 ½ years old

Thank you for the risk you take to provide our children a safe and free future. God bless and come home safe and sound.

—D.

America is a place and country that invites whomever, from wherever, makes them feel right at home, and gives them the chance to accomplish a life. My heart goes out to the brave heroes, firefighters and policemen, and my special prayer goes out to those who have lost loved ones in the tragedy. May God continue to strengthen you all and bless America! —*M. Cavanaugh & Family*

As I read through the entries in each album, these thoughts became clear: The people are with us. The Nation is with us, even way out here. Wow!

09 December
From: CHAPS@SHREVEPORT
To: RB@HOME

Subject: Good Morning! (DEC 09)

Good Morning!

We had a packed house for chapel today! Today is Hope Sunday in Advent and the community seems to be following along very well.

We are receiving tons of "Any Sailor" mail and care packages from across America. Of particular note, there is a private school in Richmond that sent us over one-hundred individually wrapped packages. The contents were from Ukrop's—which only people from the Richmond area would recognize. I suspect the CO is going to task me with drafting a bunch of "Thank You" notes for these organizations and schools, and rightly so. The flood of support is truly appreciated by the single sailors.

The rest of the day has been a holiday routine as the crew takes a breather after an exhausting week. I took this as an opportunity to write my second chapter in the deployment journal. I sent the first edition for the newspaper back in Cranford but I have yet to receive any response. I am going to send it to the Recorder as well.

Have a blessed day in worship!

Love,
Chaps

After chapel, I had brunch and went back down the library to go through more of the "Any Sailor" boxed mail. The first several packages I opened had the same contents—copious cards and letters. Then I came across a box that had some musical CDs in it. Most of it was pop tunes of the day, which really did not interest me. I dug a little deeper and found two CDs that had a collection of great Gospel and Jazz music by Mahalia Jackson and John Coltrane. I took the liberty of keeping those CDs for myself because I knew they would serve as good down time music, especially during our holiday routine.

I left the library and headed straight upstairs for my stateroom, anxious to hear some new music. All the CDs I brought with me back in September had been played so many times the music was old and no longer played. When I reached my room, I sat down at my desk, pulled out my CD player, and placed the Coltrane disc into the player.

<<Click>>

The first song, "Spiritual," began with that familiar saxophone in the lead, with slight drum rolls, muted clashing cymbals, keyboard and bass backing it up. *Coltrane...yeah, that's Coltrane!* Just the first thirty seconds or so put me in a relaxed mood. I leaned back in my chair, kicked my feet up on my desk—something I never do—and just listened, soaking up the smooth sounds of Coltrane.

It all brought me back home for a moment. In my home, my father introduced us to artists like John Coltrane, Miles Davis, Dave Brubeck, Sarah Vaughn, Ella Fitzgerald, and Nina Simone at an early age. My father was a fan of all kinds of music but he had a special fondness for Jazz. He recorded thousands of hours of it on hundreds of reel-to-reel tapes, labeling each by artist, lists of songs, and date recorded. Some of the music was recorded live during jam sessions broadcast from radio stations in New York City. At the time he made the recordings, I did not know these artists or have much of an appreciation for their music. It was only now as an adult that I understood the care and craftsmanship my father took with these recordings and how special were the artists he captured.

The next track was "Blue Train." It was better than the first! This was definitely a treat, so good I wished I could have hung a "Do Not Disturb" sign outside my hatch. I closed my eyes and let the music take me deeper.

"TATTOO, TATTOO! LIGHTS OUT IN FIVE MINUTES! STAND BY FOR THE EVENING PRAYER."

Search our Hearts

Let us pray

Search me, O God, and know my heart; test me and know my anxious thoughts. See if there is any offensive way in me and lead me in the everlasting way. (Psalm 139:23)

Lord that which you see clearly in us may not be evident to our understanding. The trials we encounter may seem more of a burden than a blessing. We may err in judgment unable or unwilling to check our course.

But we call upon you anyhow to guide us along a path that is pleasing to you. Only there we can find eternal life, eternal joy, and most importantly your approval.

Search me, O God, and know my heart. Try me and know my thoughts. See if there is any wicked way in me and lead me in the everlasting way.

Amen.

"Thanks Chaps!" said the Boatswain Mate-of-the-Watch.

"No problem. You're welcome!" I replied, hanging up the 1MC microphone. "Have a good night."

"You too, Sir!" he said, as I made my way through the darkness and out of the Pilot House. I was looking forward to hitting the rack tonight because I wanted to hear the songs on the Mahalia CD. Nothing against the artists on the contemporary Christian CDs in my collection but Mahalia Jackson was in a class by herself—rich, soul-stirring gospel music deeply rooted in the African-American church experience.

Once I made it back to my stateroom, I changed out of my uniform and put on some night clothes, changed out the Coltrane CD for Mahalia and clicked the "PLAY" button:

"How I got over
How did I make it over?

You know my soul look back and wonder
How did I make it over?

How I made it over
Comin' on over all these years

You know my soul look back and wonder
How did I make it over?

"Sing Mahalia!" I whispered.

But soon as...I can see Jesus
The man...who died for me
Man that bled and suffered
And he hung on Calvary...

I want to thank Him...for how he brought me...
And I want to thank God...for how he taught me...

And I'm gonna thank God for old time religion
And thank God for giving me vision...

I'm gonna join the heavenly choir
Gonna sing and never get tired...

Gonna thank God, thank him for being sooo good to me"[6]

---

[6] "How I got over" by Mahalia Jackson

The feeling this kind of gospel music evoked was difficult to put into words. It sort of grabbed hold and moved through me like the circulation of my own blood. It was a deep, visceral, soul-soothing sensation. This CD was a Godsend! It was easy to see how its inspiration was going to carry me through the lean days of the mid-deployment period.

"TAPS, TAPS! LIGHTS OUT! ALL HANDS TURN TO YOUR BUNKS! MAINTAIN SILENCE ABOUT THE DECKS! TAPS!"

10 December
"Double Digit" Day

I wrote my wife this morning to announce we had officially crossed a small milestone in the deployment: "Double Digit Day." We were now under one hundred days left on the deployment but I think I was probably the only one of us counting.

We met nearly every morning over email—mine sent early, her response received by mid-afternoon, which was morning on the East Coast. However, the pattern was changing. She did not project the need to answer up every day. I knew what was happening—it was the Mid-Deployment Malaise and there was nothing I could do about it.

Marines depart the Ship

The last of our Marines were scheduled to depart the ship. This time was different. We knew they were going into Afghanistan and into conflict. What we did not know was when they were coming back nor who would make it back. No one spoke of the latter point, not even the Marines.

"Fair Winds," Shipmates!

With the Marines gone, I sensed it would be a good time to increase Deckplate Ministry about the ship. Over the next few weeks I would make myself present at the latest hours of the day and most remote parts of the ship where sailors stood Watch. The whole point was to somehow bring encouragement and boost morale. The best way to accomplish this was immediately after the evening prayer.

Transitions

Let us pray.

Gracious Lord, we find ourselves preparing for another transition. We are pulling apart only to regroup and reconfigure so that our forces may be sent to other platforms and perhaps ashore in support of the mission, which at times may be executed even as the ink dries on the printed page.

Transitions tend to stretch us thin. They drain energy and resources, attention spans and patience, especially when they occur so often. We accept them, though, in part and parcel as the very nature of our business.

Lord please remain constant, consistent, and predictable, true to your Word and faithful to all your promises. Be the one sure thing in our lives that no one can change, a dependable source of comfort and peace that makes our lives make sense.

In your Strong Name we pray,

Amen.

"Thanks Boats!" I said as I hung up the microphone.

"No problem, Sir!" the Boatswain Mate-of-the-Watch replied.

Instead of hitting the rack, I decided to stay for while with the sailors on Watch in the Pilot House. I made my way over to the Navigation Table to speak with the Quartermaster-of-the-Watch.

"Hey Shipmate, how is it going?" I asked him.

"It's going, Sir," he replied. He was plotting the ship's course on the navigation chart and arose from his bent over position to engage in conversation. Navigation charts were detailed maps displaying the depth of the ocean upon which ships sail. The Quartermaster-of-the-Watch was its craftsman and keeper.

"Where are we going?" I asked.

"Nowhere fast, Sir. We are steaming a Night Box," he said.

"Gator Squares, again?" I asked

"Yes, Sir. We will be cutting squares all night," he said.

"Well, show me where we are," I said.

"Yes, Sir. Well, we were here," he said pointing to a prior position on the chart. "Now we are out here steaming a Night Box."

"So, how much area does this chart cover?" I asked. The quartermaster began to describe our position relative to Pakistan and within the North Arabian Sea. As he explained, my eyes drifted to a caption at the bottom of the chart that read:

SOUNDINGS IN FATHOMS

He continued with his explanation. Ask any Sailor about what they do for a living or, more specifically, how something works and you are in for healthy conversation.

"TAPS, TAPS, LIGHTS OUT! ALL HANDS TURN TO YOUR BUNKS. MAINTAIN SILENCE ABOUT THE DECKS. TAPS!"

I left the Navigation Table to strike up a conversation with the Officer-of-the-Deck (OOD). He was standing over the RADAR Scope with the Junior Officer-of-the-Deck (JOOD).

"How is it going OOD?" I asked.

"Fine, Sir. Just going over some surface contacts with the JOOD," he said.

"How you doing, Chaps?" asked the JOOD.

"Doing well. Seems like a quiet night tonight," I said.

"Yes Sir. Just cutting squares," she said. "See, here we are," she continued while pointing at the screen, "and here is WHIDBEY ISLAND, and here is the BATAAN. We all have a Night Box."

"Wow! BATAAN's got the biggest box," I remarked.

"Yes, she is the biggest ship and commands the widest birth," she said.

"Yep! The 'Death Star'!" interjected the OOD.

I chuckled at his comment. The "big deck" of an Amphibious Ready Group was humorously known as the "Death Star," due to its status as the mother ship and the incessant activity of air and landing craft that would transit to-and-fro from it.

After speaking with these officers, I struck up some small talk with the helmsman, the Sailor manning the wheel, and the lee helmsman, the one responsible for sending telegraphed speed orders to main control in the Engine Room. They were two junior sailors, both below the rank of E-4. I almost made it to the end of their Watch at midnight but the bed in my stateroom began to call me. So, I said goodnight to Bridge Watch and departed the Pilot House.

11 December

"REVEILLE, REVEILLE! ALL HANDS HEAVE OUT!
BREAKFAST FOR THE CREW!"

No emails this morning in my inbox from my wife. After I read through the rest of the new messages, I said a short prayer for her and our son and carried on with my day. I kept reminding myself that she was fine and if there was something wrong or she needed me, she would write.

Coming Through for Us

Let us pray.

Gracious Lord, thank you for coming through for us over and over again. We possess such great skill at what we do that we hardly flinch at the built-in hazards of our work. Even today's evolution was conducted in safety, which is always one of two possible outcomes.

Are we astute enough to notice the pattern? In all ways large and small you keep coming through for us. You prove your faithfulness at sunrise, your resounding love at "eight bells," your undying devotion at sunset, and your omnipresence under an indigo canopy of stars.

Thank you, Lord. Just simply, thank you.

Amen.

Aft Lookout

After the prayer, I headed out to Aft Lookout, one of the most solitary watches aboard the ship. A Sailor was posted outside of the ship at the far-end corner of the Starboard side of the Flight Deck. Aft Lookout was manned from Dusk to Dawn in two-hour increments. It was an important Watch, whose primary responsibility was monitoring surface contacts or threats to the ship and then reporting them to the Bridge Watch in the Pilot House.

Sailors on the Aft Lookout Watch had a sound powered phone around their neck and earphones to facilitate communication with the Bridge. It was one of those critical yet forgotten watches around the ship. No one ever visited Aft Lookout, except the Sailor who was relieving the one who was covering this Watch.

The safe route out to this Watch was to head all the way to the end of the Flight Deck one deck below on the Second Deck and emerge through a hatch at the end of the ship. The quick route was to exit the Mess Deck and walk straight out across the Flight Deck until the Sailor reached the Aft Lookout position. The problem was it was near pitch dark with little to no illumination from a waning crescent moon. It was a warm night and the breezes and the ocean were calm as I took the quick route across the Flight Deck to the watchstanding position.

Once I arrived, it was easy to strike up a conversation. I had a captive audience and the Sailor appreciated the company. I was perhaps the only human presence he would see all night, besides his Watch relief. Without the visit from the chaplain, the Sailor would monitor the seas and hypnotic wake of whitewater that was churned up from the ship's propellers.

12 December

No note from my wife again but I did get this message from back home.

From: CHERYL@THECRANFORDEAGLE
To: CHAPS@SHREVEPORT

Subj: Right back at you, my friend

Dear Chaplain Brown,

I hope this letter finds you well. You are in my prayers every day. Yes, I did receive your first submission and it was so moving, so wonderful. Thank you for sharing your thoughts so beautifully.

I broke the first installment into two parts because I thought you might not get another one to me on time. Rest assured the prayer, in its entirety was printed in the second part. I did not want to repeat it twice so I made a judgment call and broke the first part of the story as SHREVEPORT left Norfolk and the second part with you on the way to Morehead City.

I am looking forward, as are *Eagle* readers, to the next in this series. If you can, please send me the next one as soon as you are able, this week, if possible. I write your series on a Friday for the following Thursday's paper so I have enough time to ensure it is perfect.

The next edition is on the 13th of December, the following on the 20th. I was hoping that for the 20th you could give me a very special installment for our Christmas edition. I know my readers are disheartened this year, but both you and I know that through your beautiful writing we can give hope to those in pain.

This is indeed a very different Christmas season, tempered by the tragedy of September 11, almost as if the innocence has been lost. I feel it myself but I know our parents endured more hardships and we will have to as well.

I believe that we were put in each other's paths so this series could be published. It is filled with faith, hope, pain and the real side of war. But most of all, God is a part of it and the paper approved every word. I never had a doubt. This is a family-owned newspaper and they are wonderful people.

I have to go to work now. I am on a deadline. Email me and let me know when the next installment of the story will be ready. Again, God bless you and all those on the ship. My prayers are with you every day. Hope your wife and son are well. My heart aches for them and you at this time of year.

Sincerely,
Cheryl

From: CHAPS@SHREVEPORT
To: CHERYL@THECRANFORDEAGLE

Re: Right back at you, my friend

Dear Cheryl,

I am well and filled with gratitude! Thanks for initiating an effort that has been in my prayers and dreams for several months. What is happening with the Lord bringing about our meeting and the publication of this series reminds me of a scripture from the New Testament. "No eye has seen, no ear has heard, no heart has perceived what God has planned for those who love Him."[7] One day it is my hope to turn this series into a book. The scope of the novel will comprise my entire experiences aboard SHREVEPORT. Understanding this, there are a few more chapters yet to be written, all of which will be inscribed by faith trusting the Lord to reveal them to me. I suppose He wanted to give part of these experiences a preview before the work is completed. As a Christian, I am not big on coincidence; our meeting and the publication is providential.

As for future submissions, I can produce one per week if you would like, reserving special submissions like next week's (DEC 20) at appropriate times. Each submission will be about the same length and should you

---

[7] 1 Corinthians 2:9

choose to split them I can send two prayers instead of one. I will leave that to your judgment. The next submission already has something special in it for Christmas that I believe will grab the readers' attention.

Thanks again for everything you have done. May the Lord richly bless you!

Sincerely,
David Brown

Flexibility

Let us pray.

Gracious Lord, our challenge is to stay focused and flexible. To keep up the good work in spite of where it takes us.

Should we consider flexibility to be a learned quality or just endemic to our operational environment? The very notion itself is irrelevant to you. Only you have the full scope of things and are well apprised on any situation. You have already seen "check mate" long before the first pawn gives up its position.

Lord, there is no limit to the resources you could utilize to reach out to us— our variable schedule and multiple tasking included. Do as you please, O Lord, but make it possible for us to remain recipients of your protection, love, favor, and blessings in whatever direction we may head.

This we pray in your Sovereign Name,

Amen

Shaft Alley

It has been described as the most miserable Watch aboard ship. Seven decks down, watching the propeller's shaft rotate incessantly for hours upon hours. Shaft Alley was an obscure passage extending from the engine rooms all the way to the end of the ship that contains the ship's propeller shafts. Unlike Aft Lookout, Shaft Alley had to be manned round-the-clock while the ship was underway. The last three decks were a vertical ladder down a two-foot square hole.

Sailors on Watch down there monitored the bearings of the propeller shafts leading from the motors all the way to the ship's propellers at the end of the ship. The Watch would perform maintenance like check for proper lubrication of spring bearings, bearing temperatures especially during high-speed operations, and proper operation of self-oiling devices. Shaft Alley watchstanders were also required to report every hour to Main Control and immediately if abnormal conditions occurred.

The Sailor on Watch, from the Engineering Department, was surprised but pleased to see me. Again, it was easy to strike up a conversation with him seeing that I was an unexpected face-to-face contact and he seemed appreciative of my presence. I made sure I told him how much I appreciated what he was doing even though he was just doing his duty.

On the whole, the engineers were the unseen heroes of the ship. "We Carry The Load," was a slogan by which these sailors lived and it was the truth: from electricity, ventilation, propulsion, internal communications, firefighting, and producing fresh water, engineers routinely and consistently kept the ship running.

13 December
0702
From: RB@HOME
To: CHAPS@SHREVEPORT

Subj: Hi!

Hey! I received a copy of the ship's newsletter. Who took all of the pics? They are very clear. Our son pointed to your picture and kept saying "Dada" while smiling.

No other news from this end. Hey! Could you email your brother's address? I am thinking of getting his whole family a gift card from Best Buy. This way they can decide what they would like to purchase. Not many shopping days left until Christmas. I better get busy.

That is all from the home front. Will talk to you soon.

5THINGS

Our son sleeping through the night
Our son trying new foods
Our family
The way God sustains us even through difficult situations
Waking up to see another day

Love Ya!
RB

I sat for a moment and re-read her message a couple of more times. After forty-eight hours of no news, one would think there would be more to report. I just appreciated hearing from her and was reassured to know everything at home was okay.

My wife now had her own daily routine of emotional support, constructed in my absence over the past three months. The infrequency of her emails reflected this fact.

Pilot House
0915

I ventured up to the Pilot House to get some fresh air and check in with the sailors on Bridge Watch. When I entered, the captain was sitting by himself in his chair and staring through the forward windows out into the ocean. I observed him for a few moments and noticed he was in a pensive mood, not speaking to anyone, though, all were cognizant of his presence. I approached the captain from his left and greeted him.

"Good morning Sir!

"'Morning Chaplain. How is it going?" he asked.

"Things are going well, Sir," I replied. "How are you?"

"Doin' fine," he said as he continued to stare. I sensed he wanted to talk so I remained silent and stared with him. "Except," he said breaking the silence. "Something does not make sense. I was thinking back over this year about what the ship and the crew have been through. We barely passed the FEP back in the winter, the INSURV Inspection beat us up, we have had a whole bunch of things break down throughout the workups, and, of course, we are the ship that 'ran aground in the Suez' a little over a year ago. Yet, here we are. *We* are the ones out here on station, the first responders in this war. I cannot seem to reconcile all this in my mind. What you think?" he asked.

"Well, Sir," I paused for a moment to collect my thoughts. "Sometimes God takes that which is the most unlikely person or situation and causes it to be an example for all to emulate. Sometimes it is God's providence. He does this so that it would be clear that He has done it and not us."

"Hmm! I never thought of it like that," he said. "That is interesting!"

"Yes, Sir. There is even a scripture in the Bible echoing this thought," I told him.

"Well send it to me. I would like to read it for myself," he said.

"Aye, Aye, Sir! I will send it when I get back to my office." I said.

"Thanks Chaplain."

"You're welcome, Sir!"

I departed the Pilot House anxious to get to my computer and fire off that scripture to him.

From: CHAPS@SHREVEPORT
To: CO@SHREVEPORT

Subj: "Providential" Scripture

Sir,

Here is the scripture I referred to this morning. I believe it sums up what the Lord's plan was for SHREVEPORT all along and in many respects our own lives:

1 Corinthians 1:26-31 (TEV)

Now remember what you were, my friends, when God called you. From a human point of view few of you were wise or powerful or of high social standing. God purposely chose what the world considers nonsense in order to shame the wise, and he chose what the world considers weak in order to shame the powerful. He chose what the world looks down on and despises and thinks is nothing, in order to destroy what the world thinks is important. This means that no one can boast in God's presence. But God has brought you into union with Christ to be our wisdom. By him we are put right with God: we become God's holy people and are set free. So then as the scripture says, "Whoever wants to boast must boast of what the Lord has done."

Very respectfully,
Chaplain Brown

From: CO@SHREVEPORT
To: CHAPS@SHREVEPORT

Re: "Providential" Scripture

Thanks. Right on the mark!

CO

"DAILY PRAYER MEETING WILL BE HELD IN SACC AT 1230."

Jasmine approached me after the prayer meeting to ask if I had thought anymore about doing a choir concert on the Mess Deck. I had to be honest with her and admit that I had not. She did not seem deterred by my answer, though. In fact, she encouraged me to seriously consider it because she thought it would be a great way to boost morale around the ship. I promised her I would.

In my mind, there was more to this than just standing up and singing. I had to ask for volunteers, set rehearsal times, advertise in the POD. There were some moving pieces she may not be considering.

"TATTOO, TATTOO! LIGHTS OUT IN FIVE MINUTES! STAND BY FOR THE EVENING PRAYER."

New Strength

Let us pray.

O God, you are my God, and I long for you. My whole being desires you; like a dry worn out, and waterless land, my soul is thirsty for you.[8]

Lord, help us realize that when we run low on energy, our strength wanes to nothing, or our mental tank is all tapped out, you stand ready and able to fully replenish at the point of our greatest need. In such a loving way you remind us that with your presence in our lives we never have to experience any such emptiness ever again.

Fill us, Lord. Quench the thirst within.

Amen.

---

[8] Psalms 63:1

-18-

BOOSTING MORALE

Keeping spirits high

14 December 2001

"Beer Day"
Around Noon

I t's a rule: any naval vessel that is underway for forty-five consecutive days earns what is called a "Beer Day." Each member of the crew, regardless of age—some of the crew was under twenty-one—was entitled to consume two cans of beer. This rule was in place as an effort to boost morale and it could not have come to our ship at a better time.

The Supply Officer worked out a ticketed-voucher system through which each Sailor could receive their beer quota. Each division on ship received the tally of tickets from the Supply Department that matched the number of sailors in their section. The sailors would redeem their ticket at the distribution point on the Flight Deck and then have their name marked on a master roster to confirm the receipt of the beers. The beers had to be consumed in the open-air of the Flight Deck and under no circumstances brought inside the ship. Even though I did not drink alcohol, I was interested to see how the distribution of beer was going to work.

The captain decided to have a Steel Beach Picnic to coincide with Beer Day, which seemed to be an extra attempt to boost morale. It worked! The Flight Deck was flooded with hundreds of sailors, most in line to redeem their vouchers at the beer booth and then head over to the grill stations to get some food. I was slightly embarrassed by this because even I, as a crewmember, received a beer voucher from my department head. When I informed him I did not drink, he said, "Sorry, Chaps. A rule is a rule. *Every* Sailor gets a beer voucher."

"Well, what do you want me to do with it?" I asked.

"'Does not matter to me. You can use it, discard it, or give it away," he said.

"Roger that. Okay. Thanks!" I said.

I could have thrown it away but decided I would contribute to the morale effort by giving my voucher to some lucky Sailor. Then I wondered: *Can four beers make a Sailor drunk?* I did not know that answer and did not want to contribute to anyone's intoxication. I realized I was over-thinking this so I picked out a Sailor at random. "Hey Shipmate! Here. You can have my beers," I said handing him my voucher.

"Whoa! Really Sir?" he asked with surprise.

"Yes, 'cause I don't drink and it seems like it would be a waste just to throw away two good beers," I said.

"Thanks Sir! I really appreciate it," he said, grabbing the voucher and heading over to get in line for the beer booth.

It all seemed to be working. There was not a dejected face on the Flight Deck. Everyone had a can of beer in their hands—savoring each sip—and another in the side pocket of their coveralls. Levity and lightheartedness, high-fives and fist bumps, mock toasts to anything and nothing abounded; it was a splendidly planned celebration—burgers, dogs, and suds—right in the middle of the North Arabian Sea. What could be better?

"TATTOO, TATTOO! LIGHTS OUT IN FIVE MINUTES! STAND BY FOR THE EVENING PRAYER."

Second Wind

Let us pray.

Gracious Lord, we look to you tonight for a Second Wind; divine refreshment that revives our dormant spirit.

Indeed, we are proficient and smart and well experienced but we pray that these things would not block your blessing setting us Leeward of your sustaining power. Let all our plans and expectations soar under the updraft of your Spirit.

Spirit of God, move about this ship, and as you do please be ambivalent towards every compartment and ladderwell, apathetic to each hatchcoming and scuttle, oblivious to passageways and storage spaces; but place your focus on all the precious souls that move and rest and inhabit this vessel. Breathe into us a second wind, for our nation needs us alert, savvy, and swift and we need the very same from each other.

In your Strong Name we pray,

Amen.

"TAPS, TAPS, LIGHTS OUT! ALL HANDS TURN TO YOUR BUNKS. MAINTAIN SILENCE ABOUT THE DECKS. TAPS!"

15 December
0712

From: CHAPS@SHREVEPORT
To: RB@HOME

Hey!

I hope you and our son had a good night's sleep. I am just beginning my workday here in the office but I have been up since 0400 doing some deck-plate ministry. I have been getting around the ship more often to see how the sailors are doing. Some of the best conversations happen at that time of the morning or really late at night. People feel free to share what is on their minds at these times so all I have to do is show up and listen. It is amazing what they want to talk about—politics, religion, favorite foods, etc. I usually pray the Jabez prayer before I go out so the sailors would become more inclined to talk about their faith.

I have a NSAC class today. This latest group of sailors checked aboard while we have been underway. The whole point of NSAC is to keep these new sailors on the straight and narrow so they will remain that way for the rest of their time aboard ship. It has been effective thus far and I believe it will be in the future.

Have a blessed day!

Love,
Chaps

Sharpening skills

Let us pray.

Gracious Lord, thank you for today's lesson in sharpening skills.

Every time the ridged file of training runs across the mettle of our expertise, it shapes, coarse, then smooth, then to a fine polish, producing a spearhead that is sterling sharp.

We understand this refining process is not accomplished just because it is briefed on the previous evening. It takes the hard work and tireless dedication of all hands. Lord we have looked and discovered that in this mission there are no unimportant people. Everybody's best efforts count.

So surround us with your abundant favor, provide us with protection and success.

In your Merciful Name we pray,

Amen.

16 December

Just After Morning Worship

I was back in my office when this announcement came over the 1MC:

"ASSEMBLE ALL DEPARTMENT HEADS IN THE CAPTAIN'S CABIN!"

Hmm. What could this be about? By the time I made it upstairs to the captain's cabin, all of the department heads were already there, seated in chairs arranged in a school circle around Captain.

"Okay, is this everybody?" he asked around the room.

"Yes Sir!" we answered.

"Okay. I brought you all here this morning because the Supply Officer has reported a discrepancy from the Beer Day count. It seems that eighty to eighty-five more beers were consumed than there are crewmembers. Now, I want to know how this happened," he said. "This is a ship-wide incident and I mean to get to the bottom of it."

Oh boy! I know what happened. Heck! Anyone can figure out what happened.

"SUPPO (Supply Officer), was there a breakdown in the chain of custody of the beer vouchers?" he asked.

"No Sir! Each department head had a designated representative who was responsible for receiving the exact amount of vouchers for their department," said the Supply Officer.

"Then what happened?" the captain continued. "Was their negligence at the distribution point?"

"No Sir! Each Sailor that presented a voucher received exactly two beers. The master-at-arms was on hand as a witness," he said.

"Master-at-Arms, what did you see?" asked the captain.

"Sir, my sailors and I saw two beers per Sailor," said the Master-at-Arms.

"Then what happened? Did someone walk off with a few extra cases? Were duplicate vouchers made? What?! I want an answer now! Somebody tell me what the hell happened!" the captain said in frustration.

The room fell silent. The body language of my colleagues was tense. We all realized the captain was serious. We all sensed what happened but we remained silent. When I could stand it no longer, I spoke up.

"Sir, I have to confess. I gave my beer voucher to a Sailor at-random on the Flight Deck. I did it because I do not drink and I did not want my beers to go to waste. So I am responsible for two of the missing beers.

There was silence for a moment then suddenly, everyone burst out laughing.

"What? What?" I asked looking around at the laughs and smiles around the room. "No, I am serious. That is what I did!"

"Oh boy, Chaps! You really did it now," said one officer.

"Yeah, Chaps. Giving away your beer voucher? I don't know. Could be an NJP offense," said another officer.

"No, I am dead serious! That is what I did," I said in my defense.

"Ok Chaplain. It is okay," said the captain. "Now, if you could just account for the other eighty or so beers, we would be good-to-go. Do you have any idea about that?"

"No, Sir, I do not," I said feeling slightly embarrassed before my peers.

"Okay. On serious note, I want all departments to get with SUPPO and go over your numbers with him," said Captain. "SUPPO, give me a full report first thing in the morning."

"Aye, Sir", answered the Supply Officer.

"That is all!" said the captain. And with that, we began to file out of his cabin but the witty comments continued on the way out the hatch.

"You caved in, Chaps!"

"You folded under pressure, Chaps!"

"You are the prime suspect now, Chaps!"

"Yeah, whatever, *whatever*!" I said, heading down the opposite passageway. I could still hear their giggling as I turned the corner towards my stateroom.

Everybody knows what happened to those beers—Everybody! Man! They're going to have us counting strawberries next.

"DAILY PRAYER MEETING WILL BE HELD IN SACC AT 1230."

I spent most of the afternoon in my office with Admin prepping for the Mid-Deployment Marriage Seminar. As I was working on the details, I quickly realized that I missed having RP1 Bates' assistance. So, it was up to me to craft the draft, revisions, and final power point presentation, reserve the ship's classroom over two days, print rosters, worksheets and exit surveys, brief the XO on the overall plan, and compose a note to advertise it in the POD. I missed my RP.

"SWEEPERS, SWEEPERS, MAN YOUR BROOMS! GIVE THE SHIP A GOOD SWEEPDOWN BOTH FORE AND AFT! SWEEPDOWN ALL LADDERWELLS, LADDERBACKS, AND PASSAGEWAYS! HOLD ALL TRASH AND GARBAGE ON STATION!"

Surprise Blessings

Let us pray.

Gracious Lord, thank you for showing us that you have an unlimited supply of surprises blessings; good things that are intended to make our life prosper.

When you bless us out of the blue we deem it a surprise, perhaps because it is unexpected or we feel your blessings depend on how well we are living. Just when we think we have you figured out, you have revealed another facet of your love.

Thanks for all the blessings you sprinkle into our lives; may they turn our hearts to a greater expectation and understanding of you.

In your Loving Name we pray,

Amen.

17 December

Just after breakfast, I passed Jasmine in the passageway on my way down to my office. We greeted each other and I knew what she was going to ask next so I beat her to the subject.

"Hey Jasmine! I still have the singing to the sailors on the Mess Deck on my mind. It is just that I have had a lot on my plate," I said. "I promise I will get to it soon."

"No worries, Chaplain," she said. "I know you are busy."

"Thanks for understanding. 'Talk to you soon," I said.

"Bye Chaplain," she said.

As I continued on to my office I thought to myself that it would be best just to focus on the one Christmas concert. It just seemed it would have the most impact if it was done like that. I reasoned that I would talk to Jasmine first but then announce my plan to the rest of the believers at the Daily Prayer Meeting.

At my desk, I began to scan through the list of emails that had stacked up overnight. I put off going through all of them because my priority for this morning was composing the POD Note announcing the Mid-Deployment Marriage Seminar. It was just two days from now and I wanted to give it maximum exposure around the ship. I started typing:

MID-DEPLOYMENT MARRIAGE SEMINAR: A ninety-minute seminar for any married Sailor or Marine who may be experiencing unexpected changes in communication with their spouse. The seminar will be held...

"CHAPLAIN BROWN, YOUR PRESENCE IS REQUESTED IN THE CAPTAIN'S CABIN."

That's strange! What in the world does the captain want? I bet he is looking for a full brief on the marriage seminar. I was not certain but I grabbed my notebook, a pen, and quickly made my way back upstairs—four decks— paused for a moment to catch my breath, and then knocked on his hatch.

"Enter!" he said from behind the hatch.

"Yes, Sir. You wanted to see me?" I asked.

"Yes, have a seat," he said.

"Yes Sir," I said taking a seat.

"Chaplain, I have been thinking. I know that you have formed a choir and you are planning a Christmas Concert. Is that right?" he asked.

"Yes Sir, that is correct. The concert will take place on December 22nd on the Mess Deck," I said.

"Well, here is what I want you to do: Start singing now on the Mess Deck during the lunch hours. I am sensing the crew is a bit down and a performance of your singing could boost their morale," he said.

"Ah, yes Sir," I said. "I will let the choir know today at Daily Prayer Meeting and we perhaps we can start Wednesday or Thursday. Would that be okay, Sir?"

"Absolutely!" he said. "Thanks for being flexible, Chaplain."

"No problem, Sir. I will get right on it," I said.

"Thanks," he said. "That's all."

"Yes, Sir."

Once I closed his hatch behind me I paused, closed my eyes, and spoke to the Lord. *Okay, okay, I hear you, Lord. I hear you.* I was convicted. I began to realize that God had been speaking through Jasmine all along about this but I just was not listening. My pride had gotten the best of me. Singing on the Mess Deck was not my idea so I never took it seriously.

Forgive me, Lord.

He now had my full attention.

"DAILY PRAYER MEETING WILL BE HELD IN SACC AT 1230."

After opening in prayer, I spoke to all the participants about the captain's desire to have us sing Christmas songs now on the Mess Deck instead of waiting until the concert. They were very receptive to the idea and thought it was a great way to share the joy of the Lord during this season. Of course, Jasmine was the most excited about the news.

"Wow, Chaplain! It is like the Holy Spirit already knew what the crew needed," she said gladly.

"Yes, He always does," I said to her as well as the group. "So let's take the rest of our meeting to rehearse the songs. The captain wants us to start singing by Thursday." They all agreed they were ready to sing.

From: CHAPS@SHREVEPORT
To: RB@HOME

Subject: My day is coming to a close

Hey!

The day is almost done. In about a half hour I am headed to the Pilot House to deliver the Evening Prayer and then I am hitting the rack.

One surprise development today was when the captain asked me to get the Daily Prayer Meeting Choir singing on the Mess Deck right away. Even though the concert is on Saturday, he thought a surprise concert during lunch would boost the morale of the crew. Please pray that we would be in one accord and that God would use us to reach people for him as well as lift their spirits.

Give our son a hug and kiss for me.

5THINGS

Knowing Jesus
Serving Jesus
Loving Jesus
Obeying Jesus
Just Jesus

Love,
Chaps

Prayer for Coverage

Let us pray.

Gracious Lord, we offer a prayer for coverage this evening.

Shield us with your protection, for the hazards of our work abound and though risk is present, we realize it is acceptable and inherent.

Surround us with your peace, for the days at sea are piling up and can create great anxiety causing us to become short with our shipmates or Shadow Box with despair.

Envelop us with your favor, for the unknown variables would seek to stack the odds against us and perhaps put our mission in jeopardy.

Blanket us with your blessings, for they are constant reminders of your presence and love. They keep our hearts filled with encouragement and brimming with hope.

This we pray in your Blessed Name,

Amen.

HALFWAY DAY

Keep your eyes off the calendar

19 December 2001
"Halfway Day" (ninety days into the deployment)

In a way, it was fitting to commence the Mid-Deployment Marriage Seminar today, even though I never planned it that way. My intention for the participants was to gain a better understanding of how all the factors of a deployed experience can change the nature of any relationship, specifically marriage.

The morning session had good participation—fifteen sailors. I began with distributing the worksheets and pens and then explained to them the overall format of the seminar. We used power point slides that depicted the stages of deployment—from Pre-deployment to Return and Reunion. At each stage, the sailors used their worksheets to record their observations and discuss their findings. The "ah-ha!" moment for the group came when we got to the Mid-Deployment slide. I pointed out to the sailors that the drastic change in communication from their wives was due to the new routine and emotional support system the wives had to form in their absence. I stressed how normal it was and that all of us, in one shape or form, were experiencing this very thing. Most of the Sailors seemed relieved to learn this. On the last slide, I emphasized they were all coming home to a new relationship, that is, they and their wives will have been changed by the deployment and it was up to both parties to anticipate and adjust to the difference.

The exit surveys from the seminar were pretty positive. I asked the group before they departed to also send me a short email about this experience so I could give the captain some feedback.

The afternoon session of the marriage seminar went well. We had a smaller group this time—ten sailors—but they paid attention and participated in the discussion. With positive comments from the surveys and potential email responses, I believed I could convince Captain to hold another session of the seminar, perhaps before Christmas.

"TATTOO, TATTOO! LIGHTS OUT IN FIVE MINUTES! STAND BY FOR THE EVENING PRAYER."

Walk with Us (Halfway Point)

Let us pray.

Gracious Lord, you have blessed us in ways so numerous that our frail memories have lost count. You have been with us through the first ninety days of this deployment; continue to walk with us through the next.

Walk with us, lest our emotions ambush and our strength fail us.
Walk with us, lest our pride prompts us into folly or inattention incurs injury.

Walk with us, in our private moments where our true essence and identity reside.
Walk with us through the emerging warmth of the dawn, declining light of the evening, and pervading cool of the night.

Walk with us, Dear Lord, so we will know that this life's journey was never meant to be solitary sojourn but a spiritual partnership that commences here and lasts forever.

In your Abiding Name we pray,

Amen.

20 December
Singing on the Mess Deck
Around 1130

We had some competition for our singing: hundreds of sailors already in place, in line to receive their food, seated and eating, laughing-talking at the tables, and returning their trays to the scullery and many others just moving about the decks. It was the height of the lunch hour and the noise level was high. I was a bit anxious about this and also more sensitive because we had to grab their attention and sing over all the commotion. Fortunately, sailors from the Internal Communications Division had set up a stand-alone microphone and stereo speakers raised by stands that placed them about five feet above the deck on the starboard side of the ship. Our group, fifteen in all, was formed in a single file semi-circle with Chief Ducass on one end and First Lieutenant Adams on the other. Jasmine was just a Sailor away from me to my right.

We began with "We Wish You a Merry Christmas," which caught the attention and quieted the commotion just with the first chorus of the song. The sailors kept eating but would glance and listen for a moment between bites. They gave us a good round of applause once we were finished. That broke the tension for me as well as for the others. "Silent Night" followed and "Joy to the World" closed out the performance. In my parting comments, I mentioned they could attend the full concert of songs right here on Saturday night. The Spirit, Jasmine, and the captain were right. Singing did lift the sailors' spirits, even just for a moment.

"SWEEPERS, SWEEPERS, MAN YOUR BROOMS! GIVE THE SHIP A GOOD SWEEPDOWN BOTH FORE AND AFT! SWEEPDOWN ALL LADDERWELLS, LADDERBACKS, AND PASSAGEWAYS! HOLD ALL TRASH AND GARBAGE ON STATION!"

I went back to my office to check my emails and found I had received several responses from the sailors who attended the marriage seminar:

I really enjoyed the class! It gave me some time to reflect on exactly what type of relationship I had, have, and will have with my wife and newborn baby. Thank you for taking the time to share the information with me. —*Chief Ozbun*

I learned a lot from your seminar and I will use the information to help ease the differences that may occur because of the time of separation during deployment. We will both need to have good communication when we are reunited and you have given us the key to that happening. Thank you! I hope it helps others that attended as it has helped me. —*Petty Officer Fasinella*

It was very helpful. I shared what I learned with my wife...she said, "Keep learning!" —*Seaman Huval*

Thank you very much for the seminar. The brief that you presented had a lot of similarities to my situation. Now I have to be supportive and just hopeful. Thanks again! —*Petty Officer Martinez*

Your seminar was very helpful in helping me understand what to expect when I get home. I was already pretty sure on what to expect, but this seminar helped me better understand how to behave when I get back. —*Gunner's Mate Nichols*

Perfect! I was pleased but not surprised with the responses. I had much of the same response from the Marines three years ago in Okinawa. This was exactly the kind of feedback the captain was going to appreciate hearing.

"TATTOO, TATTOO! LIGHTS OUT IN FIVE MINUTES! STAND BY FOR THE EVENING PRAYER."

Freedom

Let us pray.

Gracious Lord, we realize that freedom is our most precious commodity. In fact, we have sailed this far from home just to defend it and we praise you that our nation's highest ideals are congruent with it.

But you have also granted us freedom of choice, specifically that ability to ignore or choose your presence. For the former, peace and happiness may be primarily dependent upon other people or circumstances beyond our control. Life may be relegated to a vacuous pursuit of self-aggrandizement for the sake of prestige.

The latter decision allows abundant blessings of peace, purpose, and joy to flow freely into our lives. Then good fortune literally falls out of the sky on our behalf. Choosing you gives us more than we could ever imagine or obtain on our own.

Lord, either way you respect our freedom, especially our freedom of choice. Should we listen carefully this evening and hear your voice tugging at our hearts, we pray we would be persuaded to freely respond to your call and enjoy all the fruitful benefits of our choice.

In your Merciful Name we pray,

Amen.

21 December

Our last impromptu concert was at noon on the Mess Deck. It had the same hearty reception from the crew as yesterday's event. It definitely boosted morale for the moment but I wondered if these two days of singing on the Mess Deck would make tomorrow night's formal concert anti-climactic.

Request from a Sailor

From: ET3WANE@SHREVEPORT
To: CHAPS@SHREVEPORT

Subj: A Prayer

Hey Chaplain! I was wondering if you could read this tonight for the Evening Prayer. Thank You.

V/r,
Petty Officer Wane

Prayer to End the Day

 As the sunset fades into the horizon, our day of activities fades as well. We cherish these quiet moments to reflect upon our day—how it began and what we made of the situations that came our way. We are grateful to have shared this day out to sea with the ones we know and get along with rather than people we do not know, with ample feed and shelter, and good friends to lighten the day's burdens. May we forgive one another's failings—the unkind word or forgotten "Thank You." As the darkness closes in around us, Lord, I ask you to bless and protect our homes and all who are dear to us. Amen.

From: CHAPS@SHREVEPORT
To: ET3WANE@SHREVEPORT

Re: A Prayer

Petty Officer Wane,

Thanks for submitting the prayer!

The Evening Prayer at Sea is a seafaring tradition that dates back to the beginning of our Navy. Chaplains on the earliest "Wooden Hulls" would be called upon each night at sea to deliver a prayer asking for God's blessing and favor upon the entire crew. As a Navy Chaplain assigned to this ship, I have enjoyed the distinct privilege of maintaining this tradition and it is one that I take very seriously. That sacred moment at "Tattoo" is God's time to reach the heart of the crew and so I guard it jealously.

There are other sailors who have made the same request as you have but have done so in the spur of the moment to draw attention to them. If you have been listening, none of those sailors have ever touched the 1MC while I have been aboard. However, I see a genuine and earnest interest in your request, which is exemplified by the words and thoughts conveyed in your prayer. So, I have decided to use your prayer this evening but I will edit it as the Holy Spirit leads me.

Thanks again!

Respectfully,
Chaplain Brown

P.S. – I will send you a copy of the prayer after I have delivered it.

Mail Call

As Providence would have it, I received a care package from my family—right in time for Christmas. It was filled with sweets and treats as well as other items that would keep my morale high for days to come. All the presents I sent from Italy for my family were with my wife and I was sure she already sent them in time for the holiday.

Prayer at Day's End

Let us pray.

Gracious Lord, much of the ship's activity has faded along with the sunset deep into the night horizon. So, we cherish these quiet moments to reflect upon our day—how it began and what we made of the situations that came our way. We are grateful to have shared this day out at sea with our shipmates, with ample food and shelter, and plenty of laughter to lighten the day's burdens and accentuate its joys.

May we forgive one another's failings—the unkind word or forgotten "Thank You"—even as you have forgiven us. May we always have courage to deal with the things that concern us and are pertinent to the mission. Help us grow in every aspect and develop strength for future challenges.

Lord, the darkness has closed in all around and we ask you to bless us and protect our lives and all who are dear to us. Keep us in your everlasting care.

Amen.

"TAPS, TAPS, LIGHTS OUT! ALL HANDS TURN TO YOUR BUNKS. MAINTAIN SILENCE ABOUT THE DECKS. TAPS!"

24 December
Christmas Eve

We were able to hold one last session of the marriage seminar this morning and I received an email response from a participant that sort of put an exclamation point on its impact.

I just left the marriage seminar and like most of the crew that has not attended, I figured I knew exactly what I was going to be coming home to and how to adjust to it. But what I failed to realize was that I am in fact coming home to a "New Relationship." Each of us that are involved with someone is coming home to this. Whether you are married, engaged, or in a relationship, I suggest you attend this seminar.

This was one of the most enriching hours of this deployment. Part of the reason why we are out here is because we love what we do. So why not take ninety minutes to spruce up your relationship with that someone who provides you the love and support to do what you love? I know, people say "I have been deployed a million times and things are not different when I come home." I say you have never been deployed in 2001-2002, at sea for 95 percent of the deployment, and involved in a war. So think about it! —OS1 Davidson

The captain appreciated the survey results as well as the email comments. I had his full support in advertising the seminar throughout the ship. At this point, I think any efforts—formal or informal—that boosted morale were welcome. I took his advice, though by sending a message to all department heads so other sailors could attend the next sessions. Because of its name, the seminar had a shelf life of one to two more weeks. It would be too hard to market something referred to as "Mid-Deployment" when we officially passed that point.

From: CHAPS@SHREVEPORT
To: RB@HOME

Subj: Merry Christmas!

MERRY CHRISTMAS EVERYONE!

Thank you for all the wonderful presents you sent my way. It made "Christmas at Sea" very special. I wish I could be there to celebrate with you but I know you understand why I cannot.

We had a very good concert on the Mess Deck on Saturday night. We are planning a very sacred Candlelight Vigil Service and a service on Christmas Day. The Wardroom is having a formal meal for tomorrow night's dinner. We are all looking forward to the cooks making something delicious!

I love you all very much. Merry Christmas!

Love,
Chaps

"TATTOO, TATTOO! LIGHTS OUT IN FIVE MINUTES! STAND BY FOR THE EVENING PRAYER."

Christmas Eve

Let us pray.

Almighty God, we ponder your great love towards us this Christmas Eve. To be certain, our thoughts are also focused upon things sentimental, everything and everyone we consider so sweet, familiar, and dear.

We want to recognize that we are the benefactors of the most powerful force in the universe—your love. So powerful was your love that it left its lofty position in eternity, propelled itself through space and time, and took on the form of a child. The impact of this awesome act of affection still reverberates throughout history. Its evidence is recorded on every Date Time Group, newspaper, Plan-of-the-Day, birth certificate, and each New Year's celebration. Christmas Eve always provides tangible proof that there is nothing that can separate us from your love.

Thank you, God, for loving us past our faults, circumstances, and current events to meet our deepest need—your presence in our lives.

In your Holy Name we pray,

Amen.

-20-

CHRISTMAS DAY
No fighting nostalgia

25 December 2001

How does a Sailor keep from getting down on Christmas Day while deployed on a naval vessel that is over nine thousand miles from home? Simple: keep his mind on his work and the mission, the reason why we are all out here. For much of the crew this was a tall order. Christmas has a tremendous homestead sentiment to it. That is, try bringing up the notion of the holiday disconnected from any memory sweet, familiar, or dear—a practical impossibility! In spite of this, the crew was managing well. Captain declared Christmas Day as a holiday routine which meant there would be minimal work done and no Reveille, allowing the crew to sleep as late as they wanted.

As a Christian minister though, his edict had little bearing on the volume of preparation I had. My work began in earnest on Christmas Eve. We held a wonderful Candlelight Christmas Vigil on the Mess Deck. All the tables were removed and about thirty chairs were set up in rows facing the lone table, which served as the altar. Most of the lights were turned off in order to accentuate the light of the candles in the Advent Wreath. There were five candles in all; four in the outside of the circle of the wreath and one in the middle. The four perimeter candles represented the four Sundays in the Advent Season: Preparation, Hope, Joy, and Love respectively. The lone candle in the middle represented Christmas Day. Celebrating the birth of Christ is a central event in the life of the Christian surpassed only by Easter Sunday.

The Christmas Celebration Service followed suit conveying the sacred message of the season. My sermon focused on the breakthrough power of the love of God as manifested in the birth of Christ. "God's love just will not be denied," I reminded the worship participants. "Every date on every newspaper, birth certificate, nightly news program, and at each New Year's celebration, God confirms that his love for people has superseded and surpassed the circumstantial realities of triumph and tragedy, war and peace, even time and history." Both services left me in the proper mood for Christmas; one filled with praise and humility.

I hoped my mood would be contagious, that just talking to sailors around the decks would cheer them up and keep their minds focused. However, the more I talked, the conversations eventually took a nostalgic turn towards home. I was doing okay but I could sense some were wearing down.

I went milling about the Flight Deck and noticed the weather did not feel much like Christmas, partly sunny and in the mid-seventies. I was still on a spiritual high just feeling very grateful to God for the blessing of this day. I spotted a Sailor manning the aft lookout station at the back end of the ship. As I approached his position I looked out towards the horizon and noticed the USS BATAAN was relatively close, anchored approximately five miles away. I left the Flight Deck and walked down an adjacent flight of stairs to his post. He was wearing his earphones and a sound-powered phone that allowed him to communicate with the Bridge. His binoculars rested on his chest suspended by the strap hanging around his neck.

"How is it going shipmate?" I asked.

"Fine, Sir."

"Merry Christmas to you." I continued.

"Merry Christmas to you too," he replied with some despondence. "You know, it does not feel much like Christmas, Sir."

"How so?" I asked.

"Well, it is too warm. Back home in New Jersey it is a lot cooler and all of my family is probably over my house..."

He continued to share about all the things that made Christmas for him. The more I listened, the more his conversation began to persuade me to empathize with him. And I did, but with the understanding that our sacrifice for being far away from home was not in vain and that we were doing the right thing for the country. Though my contentment was slightly shaken and my focus began to blur, my words helped give the Sailor a different perspective on his situation.

Our conversation continued talking about all things Christmas and Jersey. Then from behind I heard the sound of a jet engine and I quickly turned to the spot from where the noise came. I did not see anything at first but then my eyes caught up with the sound and motion of two F-14 Tomcats on patrol. Both jets were about three hundred feet above the surface water, side by side and about five hundred yards away. The roar of their engines now had all eyes on the Flight Deck fixed on them as they sprinted well past the ship.

"WHOAH! That was *too cool!*" exclaimed the Sailor.

"Yeah, too cool," I agreed shaking my head slightly all the while gritting my teeth in attempt to conceal a smile.

The Tomcats were now closing in fast on the BATAAN. They seemed to cover the distance between our ships in a matter of seconds. Then, in tandem, they tipped their noses to the sky and headed "upstairs," their agile ascent created a long arc piercing the layer of low-level clouds. Though hidden from sight, I followed the sound of their engines through the clouds, back over towards and then past our ship but at a few thousand feet higher.

And that was it. That was all it took. I was home. I could follow the path of the jet well out sight because I, as well as my brothers, had my father's passion for aviation. When we were just kids my father would show us the old pictures he had from his days with the Civil Air Patrol during World War II. He used to take training flights in some sort of monoplane out of Linden Airport, I believe. Anyway, my father could not afford to take his four sons to a Major League ballgame but he would bring us to Newark Airport on most weekends to watch the jet airlines take off and land. This was the old Newark Airport, now just the Air Cargo Terminal and not the three terminal behemoth that exists today. Pop would take us to the end of the terminal right up to those broad windows and point out all the different types of planes. We wondered how he could tell the difference between them. Even when we could not make it to the airport, we could still jet-watch because Cranford just happened to be near the one of the glide paths of the airlines flying in and out of Newark. This gave us even more opportunities to watch for planes.

The rest of the day my mind was on Cranford Avenue. Even as I sat eating the Christmas Meal along with the other officers, I noticed the food was seasoned just well enough to make me miss my mother's cooking. The turkey was good *but*... the macaroni and cheese was delicious *but*... the collard greens were tasty *but*... the rolls melted in my mouth *but*—you get the picture. I asked the food service assistant what the dessert selections were. "Apple Cobbler and Sweet Potato Pie," he informed me. *Sweet Potato Pie? There is just no way it could measure up to Mom's.* I asked for a piece and consumed it rather quickly never inquiring of my taste buds to compare the Navy's take on my favorite dessert with the homemade version.

Later that evening, I reflected upon my attempt to stay focused and began to justify the opposite position—it was okay to savor and cherish holiday memories. It validated the deep connection I had for family and home and also proved that I was not alone but in fellowship with the mood of the rest of the crew. Though our circumstances sought to suppress such feelings, all of the subjective meaning of Christmas fondly found its way to the surface of our thoughts.

THE FLAG

It all comes down to this

02 January 2002

Today, the entire crew had the opportunity to have their picture taken with the flag. The captain even made an announcement to the crew on the 1MC encouraging us to do so. Many sailors had already taken his advice and posed for group and individual photos so I thought it best to have a personal one taken as well. I needed to change, though, from my work coveralls into my Service Dress Blue Uniform. It would not only make for a good picture but it was the appropriate decorum for a pose with the Stars and Stripes.

The flag was on display in Damage Control Central or DC Central, as sailors know it. DC Central was the place where the ship's firefighters were based. I got dressed—ribbons, brass belt buckle, shiny shoes and all—and made my way from my stateroom down to DC Central. When I reached the door at the front of the office, I noticed two hooks embedded in a steel beam that ran the length of the overhead ceiling suspending the flag. The stripes ran vertically and the field of stars was positioned at the upper left side. There was a petty officer seated at a desk nearby who was designated as the "Flag Watch" for this afternoon. Captain created this Watch to provide round the clock security for the flag.

"Are you here for a picture, Sir?" the Petty Officer asked.

"Yes, I am."

"Well, Sir, the digital camera is being used at a pinning ceremony in the Wardroom right now. It should be back soon. Why don't you have a seat in the meantime?"

"Okay," I replied. I took a seat on the bench and rested my cover by my side. I found myself staring at the flag, looking it over closely to see if I could detect something distinctive. It was an American flag, no mistake about that, and it seemed to be four feet in width and six feet in length. The longer I stared I began to get a "response" but too faint to satisfy my search for meaning. So I arose and approached it believing that perhaps handling it would allow me to connect with its symbolic essence.

To the touch, I could detect it was made of nylon except for the canvas border at the top and the stars, each one sharply embroidered and equidistant, neatly arranged in the background of blue. Early in life, I learned that the flag represented my identity as an American, not the sole representation, but nonetheless an inescapable one. I began to ponder the most outstanding memories I had with the flag over the course of my life.

I believe that my initial encounter with the flag was in the first grade when I learned to recite the Pledge of Allegiance at Bloomingdale Elementary School. When I was ten I purchased my very first flag, an old forty-eight-star one at a garage sale on North Union Avenue. It is probably worth something today. By the sixth grade I met the pain of the flag. History classes taught that African-Americans did not receive their freedom along with the Declaration of Independence. It was granted almost one hundred years later and would be a continuing struggle for at least one hundred more.

July 4, 1976 was my most memorable observation of a mass patriotic event. The Bicentennial celebration in New York Harbor featured the parade of tall ships during the day and a fireworks display at night. In January of 1981, I was standing on Broadway on a blustery, bitter cold day when we welcomed home the Americans who had been held hostage in Iran for 444 days. The ensuing ticker-tape parade in the "Canyon of Heroes" was one of those "I was there" moments that left an indelible impression on my memory.

"Hey Sir, could you take a picture of us with the flag?" a Sailor asked, splashing my depth of thought. He had come down with five other ship-mates who wished to be in the photo as well.

"No problem. How many shots do you want?"

"One each should do."

Three out of the six sailors had cameras and I figured I had to have at least two shots, an extra one for insurance. I had an impromptu photo session on hand. None of their cameras were digital though or else I would have asked for a photo too. They made several poses and many shots were with sailors kneeling and standing, smiling and at attention; all of them gave the impression that this moment was very special.

"Hey thanks Chaps!" a few of them said as they departed.

"Sir, I am sure they will be back with the digital camera pretty soon," the Petty Officer said reassuringly. "I will give a call up to the Wardroom."

"It's no rush. I will wait." I took another look at the flag. "It is worth the wait."

With this glance, I thought of my relationship to the flag as a naval officer. It was a compulsory practice to come to attention and salute the flag at its hoisting and retiring aboard ship. The National Ensign was due this basic military honor. I have even had the particular privilege of honoring my father, a Korean War veteran, as both son and Navy Chaplain by delivering his folded flag into my mother's hands at his funeral.

"Hey Chaps! Have you seen the signatures?" the Petty Officer asked.

"No, I have not. Where are they?"

"Come take a look." Walking towards the flag the Petty Officer reached up and unhooked it from the upper left corner with his left hand and folded it back across his chest. "Take a look," he invited.

I moved closer and noticed three signatures clearly inscribed in felt marker on the canvas border. The first one on the left read, "Rudolph W. Guiliani," the second, "George Pataki," and the third which was beneath the other two, "Fire Department New York-Division 1 World Trade Center September 11, 2001 New York City, USA."

Yes, this one *was* special; it honored the blood of the Innocents and represented the new cause of a nation.

"Ground Zero" Flag

Flag of Remembrance

Let us pray.

Gracious Lord, compel us as a crew to take a moment to gaze upon the "Ground Zero" Flag. Suspended and unfurled, it speaks for all those lost whose voices have been silenced, first in horror and now in memoriam— an utterance so pregnant with emotion the heart fails to contain it.

Help us look deeper than the stars and stripes in their apparent grandeur to consider the ground over which it has flown, the hands it has passed, the innocent lives it marks, and the message it resounds. "Never forget, freedom isn't free."

Lord, let this flag be more than a token of patriotism but a reminder of the frailty and sanctity of life to teach that every day is a gift from you, sanctioned and ordained for your Sovereign purpose.

Amen.

"TAPS, TAPS, LIGHTS OUT! ALL HANDS TURN TO YOUR BUNKS. MAINTAIN SILENCE ABOUT THE DECKS. TAPS!"

EPILOGUE

*F*inish the Journey! In *"Spirit Soundings Volume III: The Return to America"*, *Chaplain David Reid Brown, Commander, U.S. Navy (Ret.) concludes this inspirational story with the heartfelt account of homecoming to America. Follow the crew of the USS SHREVEPORT as they diligently work their way home to a hero's welcome.*

ABOUT THE AUTHOR

David Reid Brown is an Itinerant Elder in the African Methodist Episcopal Church and a retired Navy Chaplain with twenty-one years of Active Duty service. He is preparing to plant a church, *Hale Ho'onani* ("House of Praise") *Fellowship,* on the Windward side of the island of O'ahu, Hawaii. He is also pursing a Master's Degree in Education with an aspiration of becoming a schoolteacher.